D0978297

The Least Cricket *of* Evening

Robert Vivian

UNIVERSITY OF NEBRASKA PRESS

LINCOLN AND LONDON

© 2011 by Robert
Vivian. All rights reserved.
Manufactured in the
United States of America.

Library of Congress
Cataloging-in
Publication Data
Vivian, Robert, 1967–
The least cricket of
evening / Robert Vivian.
p. cm. Essays.
ISBN 978-0-8032-3431-4
(pbk. : alk. paper)
I. Title.
PS3572.I875L43 2011
814'.54 — dc22
2011021829

Set in Vendetta
by Bob Reitz.
Designed by
Nathan Putens.

This book is dedicated to

Sue William Silverman,

whose generosity of spirit

is a light unto itself

What was said to the rose that made it open
was said to me here in my chest.

RUMI
Translated by Coleman Banks

Here is an unspeakable secret:
Paradise is all around us and
we do not understand.

THOMAS MERTON
Conjectures of a Guilty Bystander

Contents

Acknowledgments

Grateful acknowledgment is made to the following
publications in which these essays first appeared, in
some cases in slightly different form:

"How Gunshots Became a Comfort to Me": *Shadowbox*
"Falling into the Arms of a Dervish": *Avatar Review*
"Town": *Ecotone*
"Notes from the Konukevi": *Paradigm*
"Why I Go North": *Prick of the Spindle*
"Fog Sleepers": *Massachusetts Review*
"Ghost Hallway": *Fugue*
"Ashtray County": *North American Review*
"Death of a Shortstop": *Mid-American Review*
"Casino Love": *Water~Stone*
"Gestures in Waiting": *Tiny Lights* and *Janus Head*
"Looking for the Bishop": *Prairie Schooner*
"Doctor Whisper": *Georgia Review*
"Beggar on the Danube": *Redwood Coast Review*
"Starlight in a Spoon": *Marlboro Review*
"These Faces": *RiverTeeth*
"Bus Stop Elegy": *Another Chicago Magazine*
"Washed Away": *Words*
"Everyday a Flower Opens": *Puerto del Sol*
"Walking with Marisa": *Hunger Mountain*
"Guardian of the Lost Bell": *Color Wheel*
"Hotel Auschwitz": *First Intensity*
"Working in the Jewish Cemetery": *Ascent*
"Hearing Trains": *Silent City*
"The Latecomer to Glorious Places": *Upstreet*

The *Least Cricket* of *Evening*

1

Hauntings

Ghost Hallway

I live in a ghost hallway. They come and go whenever they want,
like the transparent, blow-away wings of bees. Their spirits
hover inside this house on Mechanic Street like a twilight hue
filling a wine glass. I live more or less inside their moods, which
they carry behind them in traces of light that flood the panes
one window at a time and in the creaky flutes of rusty hinges.
The ghosts don't say "boo" and they don't swing chains.
They're good ghosts as far as I can tell, calm as a cup of tea,
considerate and watchful and able to pay attention to the least
thing for hours.

I like how they watch me read without telling me what to
think; I like how they touch my mind with ghost memories,
laughing and smoking on the porch with their neighbors. I like
how they stared out these same windows, serious and alone
in their own thoughts, unable to share with each other the
deepest parts of themselves because the inner commotion was
too great to put into words. I see how after a fight or a death in
the family they sat by themselves in the living room, wanting
things to be good again, wanting to be healed but not being
able to do anything but wait.

What they have left behind is shorn of all eventfulness as if
what happened here long ago in this quasi-dilapidated shotgun
house still lingers on as after- tone, slowly turning into something else, the echo of their memories which I navigate now

with a cup of coffee and a three-day beard. I'm doing a soft-shoe in my slippers through their long recollections, the fog that hangs in the trees between dreams. They heard the same front door whine and clatter and the soft thudding of footfalls on the sidewalk: they heard the wind in the trees and the wash of rain tearing through them on its way to another season carrying a hundred small deaths in its wake. Their senses are alive in mine, just as mine are remade in the memory of theirs. It's a mysterious transference that I do not understand. I don't necessarily like to feel the pangs of sorrow the woman felt, beetling up and down her spine like a slug of mercury, finding her defenseless in her own house at different times in her life, like a painful sickness that keeps coming back. I don't know why she was sad, but her sadness cleaned out the closets and touched the cobwebs lifting themselves out of the corners.

I think her sadness gave way to something else, something precious and loving whose slender and tender roots are planted in the long-lived acceptance of a silent struggle. Now I think this acceptance is her legacy to me and anyone else who happens to live here, a gift she blows like a kiss from the other side. She is here and not here, a mid-Michigan wife who did her duty and loved her children, though they left her anyway, and her difficult husband, who died before her. It's her house or no one's, though she never worked outside the home. Her husband is a different story, downstairs in the basement with his tools and the dark anger that never left him, his lust seething into the glue between two-by-fours, into the hammer and the clay pipe that he sucked on obsessively. His hard gray beard was peppered with roots of black hair and he liked off-color jokes. But he loved his wife, he did, and he made sure there was food on the table, and every two or three years or so they rented a cabin on a lake in northern Michigan, and then he was wise and gentle, at least for a few days. And what more could you ask for, then or now? What more could you expect without education or much money? That was their life together, he downstairs working his frustration into wood and she upstairs, mending and cooking and walking lightly though he couldn't hear her anyway with all that hammering, sawing, and moving about. He never really knew her, that much is clear; he never knew her. And how do I know this?

Some days I look out the same window and sense her next to me or looking over my shoulder. She wraps her ghost fingers around mine, like a saintly dead aunt. Everything is okay. Everything is fine. I am supposed to believe her somehow. I say the okays to myself, breathe them through my teeth, and she fills the air with the shapes of those words. How do you know? I want to ask her, but she won't say anything. The question comes later, when the okays have gone the way of falling leaves and I feel a bit haggard around the edges. I thought I was a blank slate, starting over here in this depressed Michigan town. I thought the cost of loving was equal somehow, that whom-ever and whatever I loved would come back to me in equal measure, quid pro quo, but now I think I was wrong, dead wrong, that I've been living in blind ignorance with a thread of this same love leading me from one place to another without my even knowing it, a kid pulled by a string while preoccupied with a hundred other things, ranting and raving, crying and praying, laughing and sighing the whole way in the endless, appalling chant, I want this, I want that, while the thread of this love keeps pulling him along no matter what he does. It's not quid pro quo but pro bono, free for the loving, free for the asking, because that's the way it is if only I would sit down and let it flood my whole being. She knows that already, Betty, Agnes, or Sue; she's been waiting for me all my life, my kindly, ghostly benefactor, the woman who had shoulders like mounds of softly shaped dough.

I realize how odd this all sounds, to admit to anyone, even to myself, that I live in a ghost hallway, moving from room to room, but nonetheless it's true; I hear them in the leaky faucet and see their faces in the paneled walls where the tawny grains of paneled wood stare back at me like the mirrors of trees. I see him as potbellied and drawing contentedly at his pipe while she is in the kitchen washing dishes. There was nothing politically correct about them, nothing to suggest she would ever do anything else but what he wanted. He stares out the window, counting his chickens before they're hatched. He had a hard life, but a good one, too. But mostly hard. The real issue now is how the light comes in at certain crucial intervals, filling the house, the windows that need cleaning, and lead out to the sun going down over the tops of trees; the real issue is those who lived here and how I feel their presence like a calm benediction blessing this house in the tone where I now live, how we can feel our silent and invisible messengers and what they have given us like a sealed envelope that we will someday pass on to others. If I feel their presence in strange and subtle things, the least I can do is admit it; the least I can do is to say that these things are true, that we do live among ghosts and that they shape the tones of our lives like the chimes of faraway bells.

But this is the first time I've admitted to myself that I live among ghosts. I have fought the impulse for months, for years, thinking to myself that such an admission bordered on the crazy, the fantastic, the frankly absurd; but now I want to hunker down and swap silences, want to let them know I know that they are there. And that is all. Because someday I will slip into ghosthood myself; I will pass out of my body like a wisp of smoke and look back at it and feel nothing, leaving a husk

or shell behind. I will be the ghost for someone else, someone
with his or her fair share of joy and anguish, slowly growing
into another form. Maybe then I'll be able to thank the people
on Mechanic Street firsthand, in a way befitting their calm
benefaction, for the tone they provided me to live inside like
a bell. I realize that I live inside the tone of this love that they
prepared for me, that it cradles me each day whether I notice
it or not; that nothing gentle is ever lost but is transmuted
into light filling the windows, the peace of a place, its soft and
rough fabrics, its darkish hues. I like how they hang in the
wind chimes and play their own version of *Silent Night*, how
the woman has to keep herself from humming out loud. I like
how they notice the drift of the motes that fill their seeing with
eternity, that carry what they used to be and what they are now
beyond the boundaries of promise. We respect each other, but
they have the upper hand in wisdom and almost all-knowing,
in the fact that they are no longer weighted down by arthritic
bones or the heaviness of sagging skin. Especially the woman,
she who is my mentor in the interior life, who shows me how to
appreciate the simple things.

My sad and beautiful precursors whose lives gave way to
an incomprehensible peace, my woebegone and overworked
friends: how am I to thank you now for delivering me the
private hush of this realization? How can I give back to you a
shred of this peace that you dole out to me one precious sample
at a time, like teaspoons of honey? Each time I come home
you are here and you are not here; I see you suddenly in brief
glimpses, how you used to be, and who and what you are now,
guiding me with the thread of this peace that connects the
living and the dead. Forgive me if I misread you, if the flashes
that I see of you are inaccurate. But clearly you were here and
your presence still abides. The mystery is in the rooms of your

knowing, the tone you've left behind for others to come home to. The mystery is that your ghosthood is real, that I see you and sense you in the patched-up roof, the ceiling that sags, the way the bloom of the lamplight softens the living room where I sit as you watch over me in the keen attention of bird-watchers that never fades.

Hearing Trains

In the dark before dawn in central Michigan, I hear a train
calling in a drawn-out wail that comes out of coal dust and
memory and dandelion wine drunk from a battered tin cup;
I hear its long call passing by this small town on its way to
other towns and cities, other quiet and steady breathers who
hear it in sleep or wonder in slow awakening what this train
might mean to the ones who still lay in darkness. No matter
how often I hear them, I climb aboard each car, each train,
and ride it as far as I can to the trailing, limpid end of longing itself, to the end of the country or into the star chambers
of other dreamers who find themselves listening to their own
aching hearts, filling slowly with distance and desire. The trains
are always leaving, one by one, and they are calling for you to
follow them, just as in hearing them, you ache to find their
faraway source.

I've heard other trains in other towns, like Lincoln, Nebraska,
and Miami, Oklahoma, and they always remind me of a certain
sad wistfulness, as if they hold the hidden roots of some colos-
sus, transporting me briefly to another place where they rise up
to the roof of the world. Then I am stone-struck with stillness,
hearing it seeping down time that is not mine to share or give
away but keeps calling from the tracks that lead out of town.
The one hearing it never escapes this pull, following the train to
the only place that matters, where the heart and the ear become

one. Each town and city finally becomes itself in the blue early
dark, and the listener knows once and oh-so-briefly what it is
to mourn and celebrate something passing in the dark. Hearing
trains is like this, like a protracted farewell, which is inviting you
to get up in the dark and go away with it, wherever it may lead,
like the last, haunting impressions of someone waving goodbye.

I wonder how drug addicts and teenage runaways hear these
trains, the man who lost his wife, or any other forlorn person
whose hope is running out, if they hear them differently or at
all, if they jump the trains in their heads or reconfigure them
into their own low moaning blues. You can't hear them without
feeling something tugging at you, without going into those
wide-open spaces in the middle of your chest where they fill
with the ache of emptiness.

I woke to a train a few days ago, haunting me down the hall-
ways of my days, as I thought of places I had never been; it was
not an escape but a brief glimpse of fulfillment. When I heard
it, I was clear winter air and a plaintive wail, as it resonated in
the empty chambers inside me where nubs of corn shake in
the wind and the sky above contains a single shredded cloud
that races from home to home like a thread of smoke, a sound
penetrating the walls of rich and poor alike, all the way to the
deep inner ear where everyone is connected by the same unattainable longing.

Hearing trains can do this, if only once in a while, working on your soul like a long massage, how they touch the fine
points of your spirit like soft, black ink sinking into points
along a map. Then we sense what we could become when we
hear them, and no one is desperate or meager then, but each
one of us has hopeful ears cocked to the possibilities of praise.
Hearing them is enough to know there's a way out, even if it's

in a sound; it could take you far away if you would let it, if only
for a few moments, moving up your spine to the base of your
neck like a horn meeting a jazz player's lips.

Once in Lawrence, Kansas, I got separated from my brothers
after a long night of drinking and found myself walking the
hills at three a.m. under a cold, clear sky, the kind of winter sky
that makes everything on the ground seem poised and ready
for flight. I was drunk, but not so drunk that I could not hear a
train calling in the distance, filling the town and my own feckless wandering with something like grace. I shivered in my thin
jacket, hands thrust into my pockets, but it was my own fault;
the night air revived me, and for an hour at least, I didn't mind
not knowing where I would sleep during the remainder of
the night. I drank in the sound that registered almost uncon-
sciously, less a soundtrack playing in the background than
something corresponding to a deep interior state, as if I was
pulling something from the river.

I hauled out sadness from the dark river, the sadness I could
not share with anyone, the sadness we all carry inside until a
train comes along to raise it up briefly over the water like a huge,
gaping fish in the moonlight that prefigures every encounter we
will ever have, every midnight intimation of something fading. I
couldn't tell my brothers or anyone else what hearing this train
did to me, how I was suddenly willing to follow it anywhere, that
it didn't hook up with the frivolity of the evening or anything
else we could ever talk about, only that it was there, beyond the
town and the grain elevators and my own inadequacies.

I did not know how our lives would continue to diverge in
ways that still astonish me, that the mournful train calling in
the distance also sounded this mysterious unraveling, that we
have not since spent the night together as we did then, until we

were separated and I stumbled through blue streets and broken cornstalks in nearby fields. It was too vast to fathom what was going on inside the spaced intervals of the train calling out in the cold night, but I trusted it then and I trust it now as leading me away from my flawed life, these torn ways, the perpetual but elusive promise of wholeness. If only I could have shared this sound with them, then maybe, just maybe, we could have restored what was already then slipping away, ourselves from each other, but I know even as I write this that it's a lie: there's no way I could share the passing train with them or anyone else, no way to communicate the longing contained in the hovering notes that dissipated in the cold air like smoke. I found my vagrancy wandering the hills of Lawrence, and it has never left me, and they too, I know, wander in similar circles where each must go it alone. I slept the rest of the night in the hallway of an apartment building with my hands stuck ramrod straight in my pockets, face down in front of my brother's door upon which I never knocked and which was never opened.

I've come to wait for these calling trains like some character out of Chekhov, believing against the odds that they will somehow take me away. What a fallacy to think I could know what they mean or forebode, that they somehow hint at eternity or that I know them in some deeply personal way. Still, they evoke something wistful in me every time I hear them, as if the life I am leading is still waiting for a call to lure me out of the awful timeworn patterns into something new. For I would take them up each time, drop everything I'm doing and follow them if I only knew how, hop these blues trains in the night and ride them all the way across the continent into snow-peaked mountains and the undulations of the plains where the land drops off into the sky.

Simone Weil calls distance the soul of beauty, and what better way to know this metaphysics than aboard a train that has been calling all of my life? I am fooling myself that I am a part of them, and yet I can see myself reading a book as the miles roll by, a whole car and block of daylight all to myself on a late spring day, anonymous and free. I know the page would be bright, almost blinding, and I know I would pay attention to the least sentence, letting it fill me with stillness.

Hearing trains is like this, an audition for something else, a chance to get away, a distant calling. How many others in this town hear the trains and feel a part of themselves go with them? How many let them open the inner portholes of their minds and bodies to fill up with silence and the possibility of movement? The trains roll into towns and cities, chugging the chants of a million dreamers, and they do not stop to let anyone get on; instead they call out to the ones lying awake in the dark, alert to their own quiet breathing, as they wait for the moment to get up and walk out the door, leaving everything they have ever known behind.

Ashtray County

In Ashtray County teenagers cruise down the main drag in summer, taking up a circular and feckless route that leads them back to where they started, hunkered low in their seats and listening to rap music that takes them away to bigger and more dangerous places, some Eminem, some other home-grown rapper; the boys try out their working-class rage and the souped-up Chevys smell of marijuana. They're looking for someone or something to tee off on, a midnight walker or anyone who looks a little uncertain. The peach fuzz on their upper lips is slowly turning into stone.

Before the stores close at night, old people in the aisles push forward with their grinning Michigan mouths, smiling at you with spider veins and the grim promise of lung disease that follows them around like iron ghosts in the faint, mellow after-ring of rust. Their joints creak as they pass by, like grind-ing metal wires. The patience to feel out weather patterns is the secret province of the old widowed schoolteacher who lives next door, a thin, wisecracking woman in her nineties who has officially become my lifelong hero. She's living a private life of simple astonishment in view of her neighbors, though she's smart enough to fake it. She's on the lookout for cosmic humor and the town van that takes her shopping, each step up into it like a difficult hand of bridge. Most people drive a pickup or a van and there are almost no Hondas in sight, though every once in a while you'll see a Mercedes Benz or some other luxury car belonging to the town dentist, the town big shot. School is canceled the first day of deer season and flannel shirts break out like another kind of fall, a woolen tide that keeps on coming one chest wave at a time.

You develop a name for what you don't know and don't understand, but it's always on the tip of your tongue and just beyond your ability to say it, the place where you happened to land in the middle of Michigan, the slice of America with workers' comp on its mind. Go down and get yourself a slice of fudge pie at the Main Café, load up on carbs for the long, dark winter ahead, and watch someone's dentures collect dust on the windowsill. The cultural sophisticates among you hide the bright pins of your knowing somewhere inside your coat pocket or sleeve; stuff the knowledge in somewhere deep down and safe where no one can get stabbed by them but you. They're doing *Arsenic and Old Lace* again at the community playhouse. It's a blessing to fade in with your collars upturned, to feel the calluses on your hands and the stubble on your chin. Get hard in your countenance, chew on your fingernails if you want, they will all become you. The Thai restaurant went out of business and it's no big surprise, there's no need for exotic food like that in a county like this, certainly no market for bright, glow-ing noodles that look like they're about to start singing some strange, atonal Asian song. The bookstore stocks romance novels with wild-haired beauties draped over buff guys with abs made of steel, "Come hither" written all over their wilting faces. There's a Christian bookstore, too, with titles like *Jesus Won't Forget You* and *The Last Time You Forgot I Was Still Walking in Your Footsteps*. God is lit up in the corner like a Thomas Kinkade painting and his beard is trimmed finer than a rosebush.

You can walk most anywhere and someone is watching you,

but it's not so bad once you get used to it, good eyes and not so good, rife with the scalding of pure staring. Small American flags stream by on the roof of every other car, and you wonder if you missed some national holiday that happens every day. You love what you love and can't help it and carry it deep inside yourself like a secret hurt, a small glistening pebble of personal pain. You burnish it with the cloth of your nighttime breathing. No one else in the world can feel it but you, and yet you know that other people carry their own, that some are better at faking it, some worse, and that these peashooters of pain can't be swallowed any deeper no how, no way, so you take another sip of instant coffee. The woman who runs one of the two bars in town lives just down the street and she's thinner than a piece of crenellated cardboard, with lines all over face like grooves in a kid's volcano; her name is Mo and her house is the size of a garage. She gets drunk most nights and dances a little two-step to Bob Seger's "Old Time Rock and Roll."

What is it like to live in Ashtray County?

It's like living at the bottom of a tinfoil ashtray, only the ashes have been sucked into the lungs of a living ghost that's been kicked out of his or her house into endless rows of tree stumps. Your family won't visit you, at least for long, but it's the first real home you've ever known; you're undercover in broad daylight and no one cares where you are. The official bird is your own personal crow that waits outside JC Penney while you buy a pair of woolen socks. The parking lots in winter are windswept and bald, among the most desolate in the Northern Hemisphere, good for ice skating in your car. Trains carry nuclear waste through the center of town in graffitied boxcars with a mournful and universal wail, and the local river is

among the most polluted in the nation, carrying its fair share
of freakish fish. Most of the major industry has pulled out,
making the county even poorer, though it's already among the
nation's poorest; people are practically giving their houses away.
The closed-down Total plant no longer belches out a steady
stream of noxious fumes, but it's the first thing you see when
you pull off Highway 127. Then you dream of exhaust pipes and
the Tin Man pumping gas at the local BP, his Detroit Tigers hat
on backward.

But the weird and miraculous thing, the thing that makes
no sense because there's no dyed ink in it, no way to sign away
the deed because it makes no sense and you don't know what it
means anyway, is that you've come to love this town and county
like no place else from the vantage point of your bike on warm
spring days, pedaling around its trailer parks where children
with scabs on their knees play in the dirt. This is America,
you think, in all its rawness, bigotry, and bravery; this is the
place you must come to understand as the desperate heart
of a giant nation whose poetry is pumped over the airwaves
in infomercials, *Monday Night Football*, and torn pages from
pornographic magazines. It's a force field you've entered the
size of a small nation, a kind of ground zero that has become
your home, a series of invisible and seismic shock waves that
only the clairvoyant can see. In a house down the street an
old couple live twenty feet away from a power plant that must
buzz inside their heads like a constant swarm of personal bees,
like a radio carrying its atmosphere of constant dead air. You
wonder how they keep the humming out, how they convince
themselves they know the meaning of peace and silence, or
whether even those are things you could win someday in the
lotto sweepstakes. Because Ashtray County is bigger than you
are, bigger than your dreams of fame or the last book you read

that made you want to cry; it's larger than the dazzling grin
of a game show host or a billboard advertising cell phones.
Ashtray County is the place where you end up or try to get away
from, jean cuffs splattered with mud, the monotony of stacking pallets in a warehouse, the fog that comes every winter to
press down on the roof of your car. Ashtray County is where
America dreams itself back into reality, fields never should have
been plowed in the first place, oil barons come and go and
come again, used car lot pennants ripple in a cold, driving rain.
It's fishing in the river that the EPA has condemned, it's the
working-class bar without windows where women do not go,
the Garr Power tool plant and the Wal-Mart where old veterans
have lunch and tell war stories. It's camouflage pantsuits and
graphite drivers and single mothers who leave their farmer hus-
bands because they can't take the isolation out in the middle
of nowhere; it's catastrophic orange carpeting and paneled
walls and two-lane highways and the charming, false claim to
a Scottish heritage that was never really there in the first place,
supplanted by migrant Mexican workers. It's eggs over easy and
cinnamon rolls as big as softballs, truck-stop cafes where you
can smoke anywhere you want and mud flaps shining with the
outline of Playboy bunnies; it's people singing Johnny Cash
on karaoke night and free pool every Wednesday after five and
a single, solitary grizzled man standing in front of the scrap
yard during a downpour staring off into nowhere; it's the local
police who'll stop you if you go two miles per hour past the
speed limit and singles' night at the Baptist church.

You've landed here like a bolt at the bottom of a toolbox,
like a greasy chain on the floor of a pickup. You've landed here
without a parachute, without a spare tire, staring at your one
and only life in a jailhouse bathroom where the paint is pealing
off in brittle leaves of lead paint. If you could sing this place, if

you could do a shot of it like a boilermaker or take it into your
mouth like a French kiss and roll it around on your tongue, you
might cry out in a groan and ask how in God's name so much
love could be found even here next to the smells of frying fish
at the local VFW Post 1454, how the people you see and the
person you are merge together into one humble soul out of
the body that keeps saying over and over that it's okay to love
anywhere, any place at all, that these are in fact your people and
where you've come from; you might croon a soft savage song
made of ragged cornfields and roadkill littering the shoulders
of highways every 1.6 miles. You might someday say about this
poor and desolate part of Michigan that at least once in your
life you knew what it was to truly love an ugly and forlorn place
that some days, some days, is bathed in an unearthly light, like
the exotic locust tree whose every leaf is glowing.

Gestures in Waiting

A few years ago, I saw a man hit a large buck on I-80 in Nebraska near the Platte River, or, rather, I saw his blinking hazard lights as I approached, and then the animal, his hindquarters shattered, trying to crawl into the woods on his front hooves, so humanlike and pathetic in his crawling that the rack on his head seemed more like a gigantic, marvelous crown. The deer was making a snail's progress, but I thought I could almost hear the flint of his hooves strike the edge of the pavement. The man, like most people would in that situation, stood there in the dark not knowing what to do, or knew but was not yet resigned to carrying out the deed.

The buck wasn't going far, was, in fact, straining to move inches, two-thirds of its body slack, the kill still making its way up to his heart and head. Then I was beyond them, shooting into the dark, but this troubling tableau has never left me: the roadkill that was not yet killed, the driver looking after it in bewilderment. And I thought I knew then that what I saw was two worlds colliding, the collision resulting, as all such collisions do, in confusion, bent fenders, and death. But it is possible that for just an instant, the driver was catapulted back to a time when he did know what to do, when it sang in his blood like the purpose of his race, that he had to draw his knife across the deer's throat, but instead he stood fixed and paralyzed around his own defunct will.

What did it mean? The modern world vanished in a heartbeat behind this bewildered man standing in the fog, the
cherries of his hazard lights strobing in the dark. I thought
about what he would do, how he was suddenly thrust into a
moral crisis whose resolution was startlingly clear: to finish
what he had accidentally started, to accomplish what he had
never done; to go back to the way of blood-born mercy; to find a
way to bless the animal, to ask for its forgiveness, to return once
more to the elemental state where there was no buffer between
him and the natural world. For I could see in those flashing
seconds the doubt on his face, doubt caused by fog and fear and
the animal crawling by his hooves to return to the woods.

He didn't know what part he played for other drivers and me,
the sudden tearing away of layers. He could not take the deer and
talk to him, could not sing over him or nurse him back to health;
every second he waited the suffering went on, right in front of
his eyes, the suffering of a four-hundred-pound animal, the suffering he had caused through no ill will of his own. He alone had
the power to stop it because there was no way the rest of us could
stop and pull over for fear of causing another accident — and
how unusual this must have been, how out of keeping with the
rest of the day and the rest of his life. And now the clarity of the
situation seems like a revelation to me, the ritual unfolding and
the reason all the way back to Abraham, how the man ought to
take care of the dying deer. It was a holy highway moment, a sacrifice to our high-speed way of life. I looked back into the trailing
mist of five a.m.: by the time I reached Lincoln an hour later the
deer would be dead and the man who had killed it would never
forget it, as I have never forgotten.

Often when I am out running, I pass by a dead badger or
deer and think about the fatal collision and the death that

came quickly or took hours. I wonder how recent the killing took place and the terms of the final encounter. I can't help it. Like a dream scene without dialogue, I reenact its brief, fatal moments, knowing the conclusion before it begins.

I imagine the car swerving to avoid the animal, the sickening thud, the innocent and astonished bleat at the end of it, like a lamb calling for its mother in some godforsaken place, and the crude aftermath of blood and hemorrhaging. I carry the knowledge of the roadkill for weeks, for months, until it flowers in unexpected moments like this one. The meditation comes of its own accord, unbidden and unprompted, as if the psychic energy of the dead animal is still circling above it in a flickering horn of invisible light coming out of its body. I told myself it was just roadkill after all, a sign of our chaotic and random times. Usually the animals lie just off the road in grotesque death postures, eyes still open, the eerie sensation that they will startle as I pass and charge me before disappearing into the trees. I hear the slow wave of an approaching car at my own back and calculate the trajectory of the hit, the impact and shards of broken glass. But what troubles me now is not their numbers so much but how similar they look as they lie there, most within mere feet of the pavement, as if prescribed by some fatal rite no one has ever articulated.

They're waiting for deliverance in attitudes close to prayer or surrender, prostrate beneath the sky, waiting for the unseen to steal into their bodies and carry their spirits away, like the stealthy wind that raises the grass of their fur. They're waiting for grace, for some kind of healing balm, for something or someone to take them back to the woods of eternity, or the long-lit grasses of twilight. They're waiting for a loving hand, for someone to bless their bodies, to take their carcasses away and redeem them somehow. Surely someone, somewhere, should be

appointed to mourn them or sing their praises, some highway
shaman or holy woman? Could we not agree that something
should be done to recognize the carnage and the waste?

When I see roadkill, I think of all manners of hollowness, of
garish photographs in tabloid magazines, shattered beer bottles, cigarette butts and glass ashtrays in highway motel rooms.
I think of a blue, flickering TVin an alcoholic's room. I think of
the myriad empty things that pile up around us in daily life that
do not add hope to anything, litter blowing from landfills and
ending up as pendants in trees, shredded fan belts, debris from
the catastrophic fall that keeps on falling.

I see the semblance and spirit of this fall everywhere, in the
parking lot of K-Mart and its brief flock of blowing trash bags,
in the slashed tires behind Wal-Mart, in the broken bottle of
vodka glittering in the sun. I see it in the dead deer's face, in
the dead cat whose eyes no longer hold the wonder of marbles
or the shine of obsidian stone. I go into these eyes because I
cannot help it, spooked but fascinated for the nothing I see
there, and the curves of myself looking back from the peeled
edges of a perfect sphere. I go to the place where no one returns
and no one lives, the emptiness filling the air around me and
the animal that lay there.

When I see a roadkill I imagine an impossible scenario, a
single, nameless beam of light coming from far away, beyond
the province of radio waves and the Internet, coming to touch
the dead animal with the particles of its rays. I think of the
troubled passage of all living things in the world, those who die
unredeemed and those who live on in the hope of redemption.
Maybe, after all, this is why roadkills work their influence in
me, because there is nothing and no one to take them away but

the flies. They are so abject and abandoned after all, beneath the consideration of any one passing them on the highway. Their deaths do not matter except as obstacles and objects of disgust. But I think they are waiting for something; I think their bodies, stiff with rigor mortis, are waiting for the possibility of a faraway light.

I think the thing they wait for is almost here, just out of reach, maybe here already in the way the sun lights up the hide of a dead doe fresh from killing. I drive past her outside Alma on a lonely country road, her finely knit body delicate and slim as a sleeve of supple muscle ready for the leap, her fur glowing. No way to know how she died, only that she is here, her fine head bent a little back as if to get a better look at what she cannot see. Her lifeless eyes stare up at the sun in glass vacancy, her broken bones wait to be delivered to the place where all brokenness is healed.

Casino Love

You look for it by the nickel slots and the blackjack tables, in video screens and lounges with plastic palm trees, behind two-way mirrors and elegant stone ashtrays that rise to your hips like obelisks of moon coming out of the ground. You look for it the moment you walk through the polished glass doors and see the shining rails and miles of symmetrical carpeting with patterns like geometric dreams or an impressionist's fruit, Christmas lights falling everywhere like barely contained sparks, racing around porticoes and down carpeted steps to the hypnotic drone of the slot machines, which sing of slow attrition and the occasional ding-ding-ding of quarter jackpots, like doom tumbling down rungs of imitation gold. You look for it in a winning combination and lucky streak, to get away from something else — overdue bills or a failed relationship or boredom — but your life is still leaking away as the slot machines chant their monotone dirge that never varies from its canned and soulless song.

Where is the casino love you've heard about like a distant rumor, the love that whispers into your ear that today your luck will change and fortune will shine upon you? In the Soaring Eagle Casino in Mt. Pleasant, Michigan, no one looks especially happy, almost no one smiles, and no one seems to know why she or he is there, except to win or lose. You drive into the entrance under the gigantic aspect of two screaming eagles as

big as garages, with wingspans that could take in and devour
a family of four. The eagles are identical in their fierceness as
they face each other, their talons curved for the kill and lit up by
spotlights that illuminate every inch of their swooping bodies.
They're inches away from the quarry, and you see their fury
streamlined into taut features, as they swoop down in balls of
muscle, talon, and iron feather.

They have come from another epoch to claim their prey
with silent screams, like the gatekeepers of purgatory or hell.
You'd think their hair-raising descent would keep people out
like a primordial warning, but it's just the opposite, as car after
car drives under them on the day after New Year's. The eagles
stand guard over those who go in and those who come out, but
it's more than mere sentry duty that they enact; it's more like
frozen, ongoing plunder. Who made and fashioned these hor-
rendous birds, and what do they suggest? Is the Chippewa or
Ojibway tribe of middle Michigan laughing at the white world
by using these gigantic bald eagles as the emblems of their
economic prosperity? Who melted down the nails, bullets, fish-
hooks, and fenders to make these terrifying birds that look as
though they're a heartbeat away from clutching your hair? How
can anyone pass under them without a slight shiver of trepida-
tion, a bit of awe?

The people who come here are the same who frequent any
casino: workers with dirt under their nails wearing American
Legion caps, women with buckskin jackets and cowboy hats,
people down on their luck chain-smoking Pall Malls, aging
lounge players, bored and cadaverous dealers who look like
standing knives and ersatz high rollers with Ray-Ban sunglasses. There are the countless white-haired ladies who sit
hour after hour at the slot machines with buckets of quarters,
whose feet dangle off their stools like little kids at the drugstore

counter, grim at their task, intractable, the turkey skin of their arms wobbling as they pull the lever again and again. I look into their faces and see only the eerie green reflection bouncing off their glasses like the afterglow of meteorites fallen to earth.

I'm looking for casino love in the half-filled drinks on the counters and the limes turning a wrinkled brown, in the hair-sprayed bouffants of aging cocktail waitresses and their sad nylon stockings, in the roly-poly man at the craps table smoking a cigar the size of a chair leg, in the security people with their newscaster wires running up the back of their necks, in the two-way mirrors and the lonely dealer with the sludge of sleepless nights under his eyes. I'm looking for it in the middle-aged rock band singing cover songs and their lead singer who's probably a mother of four. I'm looking for it in the blue, opaque globes hanging from the rafters that monitor the movement of everyone on the floor like alien eyes that never blink, never tire. I look for it in the old, retired couples with waistbands rising over their bellies like creeping tides, who look like they have stepped out of a time machine, in the carpet sweepers who scan the floor for cigarette butts, in anyone or anything that can shed a ray of light or hope on the spanning yawn of this enterprise.

I'm looking for the love that would make this casino new, make it surprising, wash over it like a new day, but I've never seen it and I don't think I ever will. All I see is lung cancer and distraction, boredom and frailty, and people with lines so deeply etched into their faces it's like they're human maps of desert canyons. All I see is the other side of America wallowing in itself hour after hour, day after day, all in the name of fun and the possibility of winning an extra hundred dollars, prime rib for four bucks, and special deals for newlyweds. All I see is a guy lugging around his oxygen tank while smoking with his free hand and the worst kind of patriotism that connects Elvis and shopping to Desert Storm, to video games where you can kill Saddam Hussein and then go buy a yogurt cone.

Why do I continue to look for love in places like this? Is it possible that someone in some other casino is discovering what I have never seen or witnessed, not even the least vestige or shred? How many others come here to get away from the emptiness of their lives in the neon strobes of distraction? Where are the doves or sparrows to go with the screaming eagles? If only it were different, if only once you could see some grain of hope in the faces of people who come here. The exceptions are locked away in the casino vault, whisked away like gnomes or legends and doled out at intervals to keep us coming back and thus prevent the whole thing from implod-ing, the glitter of their stories sprinkled like stardust on the ballroom floor. Just once I'd like to see someone break out of this spiraling pattern, get on his hands and knees and weep for his sins, rent his clothes like Job, and disclaim the whole fraudulent thing, but this is just a dramatic fantasy bent to my own needs for justice, tenderness, and revenge. The truth is far more restrained and disturbing.

You look for love in the casino and sometimes think you can almost see a pale glimmer of it in something close by, the dull reflection of light off a poker chip, a man or woman sipping her cocktail who returns your glances, the way a ray of natural light filters through a window and falls on a scrap of napkin like an open palm. You see the hard-lived faces around you, faces that look kneaded out of a sorrowful dough. You see the man with the sunken-in face who is tethered to a slot machine by a string that plugs in his credit card, who knows the jig is up; you watch him on the sly from a chair twelve feet away and see that his shirt is covered with engine oil. He's tied to a slot machine like a leashed human hound, pulling the arm again and again as the string bows out from his hat. What happened to him that he is moving even now to another machine to connect his rope of debt and hope to a machine that will never save him?

You wander through the endless rows of forty-three hundred slot machines lit up like electronic tombstones, looking and waiting for love in the land without clocks. Where is it, where did it go? What would it look like if you found it? You want to see the love behind this slow-burning waste, want to feel that some sort of happiness can be found, even if it's fleeting and transitory, even if it costs you next month's rent. You want to see some example of casino love, of God himself showing favor on the brow of the downtrodden, anything to confirm that this could be the place for someone in distress or bored out of his wits — that here they really could turn their lives around, find a mate, get out of debt, buoy up out of themselves some shard of joy or praise to blow out of their hands in a gesture of sheer magnanimity. But try as you might, you can't find this love anywhere in the casino, any casino, no matter what the hour or the day or the quality of crab legs in the buffet line. You're like the rest of them who come here, praying without words for one moment, one hour of good fortune, acceptance, escape, riches. You're like anyone who walks through those glass doors, believing in your heart that you're a little different from the rest, and that maybe, just maybe, today you will hit the jackpot or pick the one horse with syllables from your mother's maiden name that can run down the elusive love you have never found and will never stop chasing.

Walking with Marisa

She's about five foot two, with a body shaped like a bird or a starving child, her stomach bowing out as if her skin is stretched around a platter of salt, with skinny limbs accentuating the bowl of her belly so that you can see right away that something isn't quite right with her body. Her hair is little more than peach fuzz, only thicker, with the frayed look of George Washington's wig, liable to blow away any second by a sudden gust, dandelion blossoms nearly gone to seed in their tiny parachutes. Her face looks like a bird's, alert and suspicious in equal degrees, a mask carved out of a totem pole, maybe because she's twenty-three and trapped in a twelve-year-old's body and sees things through the lens of chemotherapy and isolation. People say she won't live long. You get the sense that she takes in more than she lets on, that she is in fact privately considering the way people treat her and what it might mean. She's had multiple bouts of cancer treatment and bone marrow transplants and is currently in remission.

Nothing about walking with her through Krakow, Prague, and Berlin and in former Jewish sections makes much sense to me, neither the precarious state of her body nor the slow, rickety quality of her perambulations, which usually took place a few blocks back from the rest of our group. I'm not really sure why I ended up walking with her at the pace of one city block every half hour, why we walked in silence, only once in a while commenting on the weather or some other banal thing. But our walks have already come to haunt me. Maybe I was supposed to learn something from these walks, though I do not know what it is; maybe our meanderings throughout these beautiful and haunted cities are even now charged with the undertow of a painful mystery, the flashing quicksilver of pigeon feathers fluttering to the sidewalk. I do not know why I walked with her day after day through the troubled history of these cities whose murdered dead cry out precisely nothing; I do not know why our wandering took on a strange intimacy for me, as she took the train station stairs one by one, our slow progress punctuated by litter and the whistles of leaving trains, street noise, and the eternal strangeness of human faces we would never see again.

We were walking through cities of ghosts, places where people had been deported to the murder centers of eastern Europe; we were looking for who and what was no longer there, a phantom enterprise of recreation and memory, doomed to failure because of the staggering magnitude of the loss. No one among us, I think now, had any idea of the darkness of what we were trying to understand. She and I and sixteen others had come from Wroclaw, Poland, where we had been working to restore a Jewish cemetery that had been neglected for decades. There simply weren't any Jews left to take care of it, and those who remained were old and infirm so that the cemetery and many of its graves were overgrown and neglected by thick, almost impenetrable weeds that grew over toppled headstones. These were the facts behind our sojourns to these other cities where I walked with Marisa, the impetus for visiting who and what was no longer there. And the oddness of this journey began to impress itself upon me right away, for wherever we went and however we got there, I was always walking with

Marisa as if I were waiting for her to teach me something, which I realize now only in retrospect, to learn from the one among us who almost certainly would have been killed first for her deformities, the way she walked on legs that seem made out of mangled wire.

I tried to pay attention to this possibility the month we were working and traveling and to see where it might lead, for the longer I walked with her, the more apparent it became to me that our work in the cemetery and our study of the Holocaust could hardly approach what we had come to discover and to try to understand: that the endeavor of our trip, restoring a Jewish cemetery in Wroclaw and reading various accounts and theories as to why the Holocaust had happened, amounted to something so dwarfed by the fires of history that every part of it was threatened by an overwhelming silence, a bottomless emptying out in the violent uprooting and murder of millions. So I walked with Marisa, a slow and simple act of wandering through the streets where people had been taken away, following the thread she unwittingly provided by the fragile wrack of her body. I followed her even though I walked ahead of her, followed her the way people follow what they do not understand and do not recognize, followed her back to how such things begin and how they foment in the heart of an individual in any city anywhere, followed her because she was the one who provided the link between what we were studying and the perpetual state of the world, always teetering on the scales of mercy and catastrophic outrage.

She was my secret link to the world of the Holocaust, my own personal guide toward some kind of meager understanding into what had happened, which I know I will never understand, as if God were speaking through her tiny figure, her halting and mangled steps that slowed down the rest of our

group. The words of her awkward steps were painful, spoken
in muted tones of woe so soft and strange that they almost did
not have any sound, like the muffled beating of wings, like a
curtain waving back and forth in a window. God was speaking
through her body, but to my surprise no one was listening — or
rather, most dismissed what they heard, relegating it to the
neat categories of inconvenience and annoyance. I myself did
not know what I was listening for, but I realize now the tone
was always there in the teetering form of her body, speaking in
the language of a warped bicycle.

In this slight but significant way, this hairline fracture in
the great body of the world, the reality of the Holocaust, or
the factors that made it even conceivable in the first place, are
unfortunately alive and well, simmering under the surface of
daily affairs like so many rats scurrying in the dark without the
pressure of history's dark necessities. If all ages are equidistant
to God, as Leopold von Ranke once said, then the opposite
is also true: every age is also equidistant to evil, to good sub-
merged and surrounded by the ether of chaos and emptiness.
When I made this connection in some winding back alley of
Krakow, I realized that I myself was implicated in this chaos
and felt the reality of my own darkness flow by in a strong
current of pettiness, self-interest, fear, and loathing. How troubling these careening realizations, the stark and brutal truth
that no one is off the hook, that it is in fact deeply lodged like a
birthmark in every person's jawbone from the start, the first and
foremost ache that makes everyone capable of good and evil.

I do not know why, of all we had studied and seen, the
Holocaust survivors we had met, the tour through Auschwitz,
it was walking with her that brought these things into focus in
a way even the others could not. I started to suspect that the
true price for living in this world is to pay attention to who and

what is right under your nose, the kind of people you bump
into on the street, the kind of people Hitler deemed unworthy
of living. She had no idea of how my accompanying her became
for me this slow and steady fugue playing in the background,
how our wanderings took on a measure of peace in the spaces
of my heart beyond anything we had seen or heard. Sometimes
it seemed that the rest of the city, be it Prague, Krakow, or
Berlin, stood slightly above this fact on hidden stilts, that the
movement of city traffic and pedestrians, the fact of buildings
old and new, rendered unto them a private history so deep and
sharp that they fall like silver pins into an abyss that keeps on
falling so that no mortal can ever retrieve them, let alone begin
to understand what any of it could mean.

I saw us reflected in storefront windows and the mirrors of
cars, warped and oblong figures moving slowly down the block;
I saw that we were moving at the speed of history through the
labyrinthine streets of Prague where Kafka himself walked
before the deportations began. I didn't want to go any faster
than I was going with her, though we hardly said a word to
each other. All of this history, and all of this grief and suffering,
and a young woman who looked like a deformed child, and one
of her teachers who did not have the slightest clue about what
we were really learning. We were an odd pair, troubled and
incongruent, whose paths I doubt will ever cross again. But I
felt drawn to her, responsible for her, as if I were responding to
a certain quality of tone that kept drawing me back, sometimes
against my own will.

I walked with Marisa to the bud of a new leaf on the sidewalks and the yellowed, brittle edge of a newspaper in the
gutter. I walked with her around discreet piles of dog shit and
bikes padlocked to streetlights, through graffitied alleys and
cobblestone steps that resembled the kneecaps of young girls; I

walked with her into the doorways of old and new synagogues and open markets whose green peppers shined as if polished by the sun. I walked with her over sidewalks through the names of the dead, Benjamin, Sachs, and Grossman; walked with her like grim spectators to sites where everything Jewish had been burned away, replaced by a coffee store, a kiosk, a new office building. There was no place we did not walk, no human place untouched by degradation, efficiency, and the secret good act that took place at the risk of one's own life; no place where we did not witness a part of ourselves looking back as both perpetrator and victim, coward and hero. Though she will never read these words, they are a testament to the outer rim of a terrible catastrophe around which we walked as lagging spectators, students, tourists — and in our walks she alone made the facts of it real in a concrete way; she and her mangled steps and the stairs where she walked and paused to catch her breath while others rushed by her.

I learned only lately to celebrate your footsteps, to say thank you to them, to see how all the shorn hair of the dead and the living is a vast and sacred tapestry that weaves around the entire world. We walk with it at the speed of your deformed legs, to put ourselves between it and others who cannot defend themselves, to say no to the dark and terrible thing, no to the advancement of prejudice and cruelty however it comes, and to finally say yes to the beauty that must reside somewhere, caged and trapped like a small bright bird singing for her life.

The Fog Sleepers

At night along Highway 46 in central Michigan I drive through
fog deep as trees where there are no trails or footpaths, aware
that something I cannot name is following me like a heaviness
that won't go away. The fog envelopes every cubic inch of my
consciousness, pressing down on the roof and windshield,
trying to get inside. I have vague forebodings of deer bound-
ing across the road, flat tires, monotone pleas to the dead.
Headlights bloom on the horizon like slow white explosions,
petals of the same fatal white flower. I take this heaviness from
town to town, looking at the misty aureoles around each porch
light and street lamp. Something is following me, coming out
of the dark, wet night in a slow-moving mist.

My whole life has conspired to pry me open to this darkness,
layer by delicate layer — not that I may embrace what I find
there, but that I may shed myself, finally, of all that is not close
to the burning of some deep interior flicker, the one I am learning to reach for like a child holding out empty hands. Suddenly,
the glowing kernel of this light is the only thing that matters,
and I think about its sweeping rays in other places while driving along this dark highway, the wide shelves of light coming
down the valleys outside Las Vegas where my parents live, for
instance, around and between unbroken islands of shadows
moving across the hardscrabble desert floor. One glowing
cactus needle in my mother's rock garden is enough to enter the

slit-eyed singing of the world. Such is the power of this fog, that it catapults me into consideration of its opposite, that reverie, failures, even dread are reconfigured on the open road between tapped maple trees, a place where God has decided to hide in a dripping birch bud or a hubcap on the side of the road.

I remember coming to this part of the country long ago when I was six, standing eye-level at my uncle's pool table as the adults played cards at another table. The sun was a mellow, golden light, filling each window with a chardonnay hue at summer twilight. I can still sip that light if I am faithful enough, if I cleave to it with a keening heart. The table was an ocean of green, and I felt then that the surfaces of everything in the house — tables, chairs, afghans, crumpled envelopes — were charged with an energy deeper than anything I could name, the tangible eternity deeper than things. Dust motes floated in a sea of light as the adults' laughter gave them shape outside the boundaries of time. They drifted by like keyholes to other places where lives entered and vanished. I was standing in the middle of a human stream shaped by voices, and did not understand.

Then it was just the smell of an old house and a rickety porch, boards that gave ever so slightly under your weight, lending it an almost sexual heft and sagging, commensurate with two bodies yielding to each other; and it was shadows in the fields lengthening out to a flooding and mysterious orchestra carrying warped flutes and curved clarinets in the plumage of exotic hens. I stood at the pool table and listened to the grownup laughter until the walls seemed like membranes to a different kind of listening where I could almost hear the liquid particles of light rain down on the roof in so many billions of dappled drops. If I ran out the front door, I would run straight into eternity and never go back. So I stood instead at the pool table, eye-level to the slow kiss of the cue ball against the back rail. The ball moved slowly where I pushed it, and between the interval of my nudge and soft bump of the rail, people were born, died, torn apart by misery and desire, made abject in their joy, uprooted from everything they knew. These were immutable facts, as stark in their reality as rake-backed chairs.

My mother's side of the family always slept late at that house, and I wondered why this was. They slept until eleven o'clock or noon, often later. They slept as if they were born for this sleep, as if their waking hours were conspiracies against the truest part of themselves, close to a secret, private sadness no one could ever talk about, the same deep, brown-eyed sadness of the Michigan woods. I loved them in their marathon sleep, the one I could never enter or understand, and would steal into their bedrooms to look at their somnolent faces far off in dreams as if I was witnessing the slow, intimate birth of their souls. I would be the only one up for hours, and in the stillness of that big, rickety house I counted off the slow, dripping seconds of the clock, the clock always ticking in memory to open the invisible door between rooms of meaning. I would not have waked them to save their lives, nor known how, so sacred was their sleep, so far off, mysterious, and shy.

When they woke hours later, it was like the smoke of sleep still lingered around their heads, haunting them with sainthood or death. I couldn't countenance the minutes, the hours, the days they would be asleep after I woke; I couldn't cross the unfathomable barrier matting their heads and giving them purchase on immortality. I was a light sleeper, hair-triggered, a hollow, vibrating twig; and it seemed they knew how to give themselves up to sleep with such voluptuousness and ease that even now it seems related to the very fog I was driving through years later, the fog that wouldn't go away, that broomed its way over hollow and bog and made tree lines disappear like the softly shredded ends of torn paper. The fog and their Michigan sleep haunted me. I drove into it not realizing what I was getting into, back to faces and places that would not leave me alone and the private history that made them, back to sound and significance where I do not remember a single word but the murmurs of their collective tongue, the after-ring of laughter.

I have never been able to remember tiredness, or fatigue, and now I think there's a moral component to memory, that maybe I don't remember my tiredness for reasons to be revealed much later. But I remember the tiredness and sleep of others, and the way their faces became molded to something far off and wistful, the soft clay of dreams. My relatives were gentle and hushed masters of sleep who couldn't talk about their sojourns to that other place where they merged into the fog because they were of it. Would I go my entire life admiring their fealty to this awesome sleep, myself just a taut violin string always on the verge of breaking? Would I ever learn to be cool and melancholy like them instead of spilling out of my skin? They slept like smooth-skinned otters, their Michigan accents hinting that whatever else the geography of dreams may be, it includes a kind of fog no one is able to penetrate. Everyone was laughing at the card table, everyone was moving in orbit around a fixed center no one could see. Now I drive into the fog at night, and these gentle sleepers come back to me, but I can't say how or why. They simply showed up in the illuminated studs of a highway sign outside Shepherd, Michigan, but even when I knew they were there, they were already gone, back to their profound slumber, back to the fog that made them.

If I should ever go blind, only a part of me will learn how to see better. The fog teaches me this. Sometimes we need fog even if

it's just to show us the sleep of people we care about, revealing
again and again what it feels like to have a center burst into
a thousand sparks, landing here and there to flare up briefly
where there is no coherence. If you snooze you lose, the old
saying goes, but sometimes the snoozing wraps a tribe around
the same common dreams, those without beginning or end or
a single voice, just the potential fricatives of two branches rubbing in the wind. I drive into the fog to get to the other side. I'm
on the lookout for something sharp and distinct emerging from
it, a hitchhiker or a deer, a gas station floating like an island of
light, or anything whose curves and edges give me something
to drive toward or avoid in this land of smoke and memory.

I drive into the fog again down a country road when I leave a
friend's house at midnight. The fog finds me at night when I
am driving, when I am susceptible to the kind of introspection
playing a soft adagio in my head. Something is hunting me
down. The fog has the power of a god to change one's thinking,
to revitalize old prayers or to create new ones. It carries with it
intimations of death, and flows around the dashed yellow lines
like ghostly fingers beckoning me to another world. Everything
fades into it, everything becomes indistinct and mysterious,
even a stop sign at the end of an intersection. If I could see just
one night bird's glittering eyes, the world would be revealed.
Instead, I enter deeper into the fog, which hovers over the
fields like the earth's loamy exhalations, a long, pent-up sigh.
Those stringed instruments play the truest music ever composed, the music of one person's aloneness on the open road.
But always somewhere nearby, people I know and will never
know are asleep inside the fog, hearing a voice calling them
from far away, back through these clouds that obscure the cost
of memory.

40

Hotel in Auschwitz

The Hotel Glob in Auschwitz looks like a giant crenulated box thrown out of a moving train, battered and kicked around but still right side up somehow, poised on the brink of a cast-off moon vibe. The train station's just a few hundred yards away, in cahoots with the hotel in graffitied ugliness to give the whole place its otherworldly gloom.

I'm staying in one of the Glob's honeycombed chambers, a tiny, high-ceilinged room with a concrete bathroom and a bed the size of a large piece of luggage. I think I stayed here once in a dream of prison where people came and went toting crowbars. The view outside my window is a tar-paper roof half a story down with defunct turrets wrapped in trash bags that rip and sing their clear song of tearing in ragged arpeggios all night next to those same tracks leading into the station and back out again, trains click-clacking their way like a distant soundtrack playing in oblivion, beyond sadness, beyond grief, beyond anything human language has the power to name, maybe cosmic silence, maybe the riddle to all there is out in deep, empty space where every train ends up as part of an Einstein equation. Trains coming and going is the reason people come here after all, the reason they don't stay for long, the vast majority of visitors coming on bus tours from Krakow to leave after just a few hours. They want to see the tracks leading into Birkenau, the infamous tracks that gave the place its well-earned nickname of *anus mundi*.

I want to say that the ugliness of the Hotel Glob and where
it's located doom it forever as a kind of halfway house for tentative seekers and Polish businessmen on their way to Wroclaw; I
want to say it's the kind of place some KGB agent checked into
once before he disappeared, that the prevalence of its concrete
decor evokes images of interrogation rooms, double mirrors,
the bullish nape on the back of a hit man's head. I want to say
that my threadbare balcony with its waist-high pen of teetering rails is a place where people go to think about genocide
or the radioactive fallout at Chernobyl, that they look at their
unclipped fingernails for some kind of last-ditch hope, the
sudden cry of angels or the burst of a bright bird's color to
revivify the world in a single flash above the place that manufactured death to the tune of untold thousands. I want to say
all kinds of things that have only the barest, tangential meaning or no meaning at all, weather reports from the center of a
primal doubt and a new pair of shoes, the first time I visited
the Jewish Community Center in Omaha as a kid and realized
with a shock that the people I had been led to believe were so
different still played handball and argued over fouls in the lane.
But these don't really mean too much compared with the other
questions that come with the stark, simple fact of being in the
place where so many were murdered.

Who could live here after knowing what happened? And
what kind of people stay in this grim hotel on the margins of
a city that itself is on the margins of everything we know and
would rather not believe about human beings? I already know
there aren't any answers, that it's far subtler and bleaker than
that, more nuanced, as if I'm waiting for the hotel room to tell
its own personal version of the Holocaust, its walls leaning
in with the conspiratorial after- tones of another catastrophic
betrayal. Some city planner chose this spot to build a hotel after

all, probably in the sixties, the blueprints unfurled across his desk, curling up at the edges. He had to know what a hotel in Auschwitz would mean or signify, the full array of its ghoulish associations, or maybe it meant less to him than it does to people now. I see him looking out of his office some gray afternoon in the Slavic tradition of not smiling, saddled with a task no one should have to face, designing and building a full-service hotel three kilometers away from one of the twentieth century's worst atrocities. I find myself pitying him in a way that's no doubt ridiculous, out of all proportion to the building's function and purpose, his name Marek or Jan, his pitted face melancholy beyond the last flickering streetlight of his native town. It's no use heaping opprobrium on an easy target like a hotel in Auschwitz decades after the fact, and yet, and yet: something still abides that I can't quite get shut of, some strange after- tone that won't go away.

The crematoria have been shut down for sixty years now, but you can still smell something acrid in the air, wood smoke tinged with the faint waft of some unidentified chemical. The B P gas station just down the street with its weird, familiar green lighting is evocative of another unholiness, even the gas pumps whose handles resemble twisted, emaciated figures about to be bulldozed. And this is what being here does to you, everything you see or look at becomes charged with the grim images of aftermath. You want the only hotel in Auschwitz to be ugly — want it to resemble the chipped-enamel design around a well-pissed urinal, scrawled with obscenities: want it to scrape along year after year, flirting with bankruptcy, with cadaverous clerks who don't sleep and blink once every two or three hours, a ring of smoke floating above the rundown pool table in the lobby. It can't be any other way. But these are irrelevancies, useless as stepped-on tin. Because the difficult truth

is that whatever I imagine about the Holocaust and whatever
I have come to know about it collapse before the sheer weight
of its impossible significance, human ash dense as black holes,
and still something makes people like me come here who were
not even there and not even born. What good is it to dwell on
human evil as vast as this, to stay in a hotel so close to absolute
ground zero?

I think this is as close as I will ever come to any meaning
of the Holocaust, staying in this gut-shot hotel near the train
station with the sounds of trains coming and going all night,
the same sounds that give me such comfort when I'm riding on
them. The meaning is meager enough, small enough to matter
before it fades away. There's relief in this, and more than a little
shame, for I do not want to be a tourist of other people's suffering. I've already decided I'm never coming back here — twice
is more than enough — but the vow is like a threat yet to be
realized, so much hollow and earnest noise, a small dog bark-
ing at a stranger at the end of his leash. But being here does
strange things to your mind, at least, God forbid, before you
become inured to it: you see or project signs of the Holocaust
everywhere like floating seedpods of death from a blackened
cottonwood tree, anything and everything bearing the freight
of an incalculable cost. Is the tap water fit to drink? Are the
throw rugs in my room made of human hair? This strange
propensity tilts into everything you see and touch, swastikas
that are not there somehow reconfiguring themselves in the
city's rife graffiti, signs and symbols and living proof that these
things happened and are still around.

I want to report that I can't sleep at night, that the service
in the hotel is terrible, the food leached of all flavor, bland as
toast, but it's not true; I'm almost comfortable at the Hotel
Glob in my tiny room, if a bit on edge, waiting for something

I cannot name. Meanwhile, the trains pull in and out on
their appointed journeys, hauling coal and bauxite and huge
concrete slabs that look like giant mushrooms. Meanwhile,
crows and magpies squawk over the largest dead rabbit I've
ever seen behind a warehouse just beyond the building next
to the hotel. These don't tell the story or much of a story at all,
just will-o'-the-wisp details from somewhere out beyond the
nearest satellite circling in space. Last night at the Restauracja
Casablanca under the stars, a band set up under a makeshift
tent and sung Polish songs as small children danced and
clapped like they were bursting out of their skin. I sat with a
beer at a teetering picnic table close by, moved and grateful for
the sight. Middle-aged couples twirled each other around and
I had the fleeting, astonished thought that life truly does go on
no matter what has happened, miracle of miracles or histori-
cal effrontery, people dance and laugh and make love as they
always have, and I watched it as it unfolded, a voyeur of their
unfettered joy.

A hundred times you've heard that life goes on, but it's different seeing it going on here, in Auschwitz, in the place where
even the commonplace becomes a suspect in the worst of all
possible crimes. I was troubled by this, in fact almost paralyzed,
as a little Polish girl's pigtails bounced on her shoulders in
delicate flames as she jumped up and down to the music, clap-
ping her hands with the undeniable proof that she was happy
in that moment and alive without knowing what she meant to
me, a foreigner, to anyone who saw her and said yes to her happiness no matter what the circumstances. Any girl can dance,
any girl should dance, but her dancing was different, cosmic
almost, a lone, essential, radiant fact that simply was and for no
other reason.

But later at the hotel I fell asleep to the sound of streaming

trash bags rippling in the wind, torn sails wrapped around
defunct chimneys. I dreamt of a piece of paper as long as
Europe slowly getting torn in half as I lay inside some bound-
ary line that cut me off from all I knew and loved. Countries
can work like this, and so can the attempted destruction of a
race of people. I knew that in the dream and I know it now. I
woke to Polish voices arguing in the hall so thick with conso-
nants they seemed to be wading in *w*'s and *sh*'s. What were they
saying? At the Hotel Glob you must be prepared for long talks
with God that are strictly one way, to stare out onto a desolate
view, looking for the least bit of redeeming color. You must be
prepared to be on edge and a little disturbed, hoping for sleep
before something happens. You must be prepared to listen with
your whole body, even the ends of your fingertips, for the least
graze of a knuckle or the scrape of a chair. The listening goes
on forever in this doomed and godforsaken city, but you can't
hear anything beyond the usual sounds of night that could take
place anywhere else. No whispers, no voices push up from the
killing ground, but still you listen like you never have and probably never will again because the listening is all there is.

You pass by people on the streets, see mothers walking their
children, young people, punks with pastel-colored hair who
throw a look at you with a sneer, and it's not like being any
other place, because of the gas chambers, as if the entire city
stood on the crust of a blackened iceberg, ready to fall into
the ocean. There's a boom box in the lobby playing American
pop music from ten years ago, but there must be a short in
the circuits because it cuts out periodically, regular as rain. A
map of Europe takes up most of an entire wall. You wonder
if you're just another tourist, and suddenly the word is more
hateful than racist or bigot. All the while you strain your ears
for the least sound, but mostly what you hear is the wind in the

trees and traffic. The listening bears down on you, the listening shoehorns you into a kind of tense waiting. You don't even know what you're listening for. If God is silent, if the dead are silent, then you will still try to hear them, to cock your ear for the lost echo of a moan. The Star of David burns through every window though its triangles have been dismantled or disguised, lighting up the glass in prisms of ultraviolet rays. Every person you encounter is surrounded by a multitude of ghosts sheer as muslin who drift through the air. The dead look up out of the stones of the sidewalk, their eyes never blinking in one long stare that lasts forever.

But the Poles who live here have their own worries and concerns, small triumphs and sorrows, clean laundry hung out to dry from almost every apartment window. Once in a while you catch a waft of its frail loveliness, its small purses of rinsed wonder. Everywhere you look the laundry seems to be waving goodbye from a hundred windows and balconies all at once, pastel colors and floral patterns and a row of hangdog socks, laundry like so many bless-yous at the edge of the world. You notice the clothes hanging because they're everywhere, high up off the ground, flappable spirits that do their own bidding in full daylight, the sun glowing through them to make new dawns and dusks, new bright beginnings for the backs of their wearers. Their wearers' lives are like any lives anywhere, but they tread upon a skein of darkness so vast it sends out its tremors all across the world. Who will tell them what they already know, what they've heard umpteen times before? Who will claim or accuse that their lives are somehow cursed, that they drive, walk, stroll over hallowed ground, that some of their very gardens give rise to plants and flowers blooming out of Jewish faces? The fact is no one and everyone, history itself and the problematical birth of nations.

Now I think before anyone writes about the Holocaust he or she must apologize for what he's about to do; the apology must be genuine and come out of the stark realization that the one writing the words is most likely a fool or charlatan — or worse, someone trying to communicate some vicarious grief that isn't his to borrow. He must admit that anything he writes about the subject is useless (though he can't stop himself from writing it), that he knows nothing about what went on here, that he's dealing with something that towers above the efficacy of words. He must do everything in his power *not* to write about it, to tell himself in no uncertain terms that he has no right in these matters, that he's a tourist or worse, a fake and imposter, a magpie of language. He must be ashamed of himself for picking up a pen in the first place, knowing that he became a writer because he was unable to be like other people, unheroic, mostly a failure, debased and sad and driven to write because he is debased and sad. He must remind himself that others have done this before and far better than he, people who had stories to tell who were actually there and somehow lived through it, in thousands of books and movies trying to describe how it was. He must tell himself at least a few dozen times, I can't do this, I shouldn't do this, I do not want to do this. I refuse to do this. I won't do this. He must apologize to the Friedmans back in Omaha where he used to go after six-thirty mass during Lent for their famous elephant ears, the bakery redolent of warm bread and pastries, the numbered tattoos on their forearms blue as dye stamped on a concrete wall. He must go down to the depths of his motive and tear out the roots. He must make of it a holy apology and a sacrament of shame. Then and only then can he begin, only because he has to.

That's all I have to say from my homely room at the Hotel Glob, the town humming outside the window in the seismic wake of buried screams. The only two realities for this gentile American born in the late sixties is to wait and to listen in this sacred and shameful place, to listen in the waiting and to make of the waiting a new kind of listening. That is all, that is everything. But I don't hear anything beyond the shredded trash bags, the rhythmic clacking of the trains, a few footfalls that get closer, then disappear. The dead won't talk to me. God won't talk to me. But I still feel their presence somehow, the swarm of their ineffable messages. I am not worthy to hear or understand their cries anyway. And I wonder if the other guests at the Glob are like me, tense and erect in their beds and chairs, straining their ears for the least sound, hopeful that some new voice will announce a coming presence or one that is already here. It's almost a hopeful thought, almost a connection, almost the thing that says your lives and violent deaths mean so much to me, I whose ignorance will always protect me from your suffering so that it remains inviolate and untouchable, the bare, bitter fruit that feeds the silence of the ages.

Death of a Shortstop

When I heard about the shortstop, an ex-teammate, I saw the gruesome end unfold before me: not the blast itself nor the leak of a sob or whimper coming from the car, but the dust creeping after him on a lonely country road where he stopped and took the handgun from the floor. I can see the dust drifting over the car and the back of his head before he angles the gun awkwardly into his mouth and his skull becomes a mist of blood, bone, and brain. The dust must have been everywhere around him then, closing in like a fist without a hand. When I read about him in the paper, I could almost feel the dust following my eyes down the ink of the page like an invisible scroll, and then I was troubled about the purpose of a life gone wrong. We called him Wob, and he had been nice to me, a transfer from Northeastern Oklahoma Junior College, an underclassman, one who was already losing interest in the game, which I would later come to think of as my own peculiar brand of betrayal against my father; Wob alone made me feel welcome.

There was the dust of the infield at Buck Belzer Field at the University of Nebraska where we played and practiced, before I gave up my scholarship as a center fielder; and Wob, prematurely balding, light on his feet at short like a tap dancer, his accountant's spectacles belying his ability to go deep inside the hole, snatch a hard grounder backhanded, pivot and throw a heartbreaking arc back across his body to nip the runner at first. He knew that infield dirt and the ways a ball could come off it as if he had grown up on it all his life, as of course he had; we all had, in one way or another. It was a kind of birthright for anyone who played the game. That American dust, that heroic and mysterious dirt, that stays with you all the days of your life in dragged infields, at least enough for you to tell someone *I played once and almost made it to the pros.* You go back again and again to those days in summer when your whole life seemed to loom up before you in verdant promise and grandeur.

Who knew then that death's emissaries were already gathering around as Wob swept his toe in the dirt before settling in to his crouch to wait for the next pitch? The day I decided to hang it up for good, I noticed from the left-field fence a sputtering four-seater airplane a few hundred feet off the ground, fading away to the north. Later I learned it crashed and everyone aboard was killed. Was I among the last to see it go? Did they notice me shagging fly balls? Did they wave to anyone, gesture to me, curse their failing instruments or plead once and forever into the radio? How irrelevant were we to those four passengers falling out of the sky? I stood in the outfield and decided to give up the meal ticket that had gotten me into college in the first place, giving up on my dad's tacit hopes for me, to play at another level the game he loved so much. From my vantage point, nothing could have been more peaceful or final in the world, a coasting plane, catching a few last fly balls, realizing I had finally broken away to begin my life in a new direction. I never did see the plane go down, but I saw the black purling smoke lifting to the sky miles away.

But I can still see my dad standing at the fence behind third base, with his sunglasses and cool demeanor; he never missed a game unless he was out of town, and he took in everything with those dark glasses, like a town sheriff whose authority was never questioned, never missing a play or a pitch or an umpire's call. Sometimes he'd call me over between innings, telling me how to play someone: "He pulls everything" or "You're play-ing too deep for the number five hitter." I'd nod, and sprint out to my position in center field. I could turn it on just for him, believe in my heart I could run down any fly ball or cut off any line drive, that the gaps were mine, and that any runner foolish enough to try it would be thrown out at third. I played reck-lessly, especially if he was there, running into fences and giving up my body. I didn't want him to ever say, "You were dogging it out there." On the few occasions he wasn't around, I just didn't have the same kind of energy, and sometimes even wished for rainouts; the game only seemed crucial if he was watching. I could almost hear him speaking through me, talking position and strategy.

I grew up a quintessential American boy's life in the Midwest, probably like Wob, playing sports all year and goofing off with my friends during the long summer nights. We used to go to tryout camps together, just my dad and me, check into a hotel in Kansas City, and the next day I'd run, field, hit, and throw against other promising kids from all over the Midwest who made the cut in Omaha or Des Moines. I got butterflies in my stomach and couldn't sleep the night before as I listened to the hotel AC rattle and hum until morning, going over in my mind how I'd fare against the competition. My entire identity was wrapped up in running faster than some other kid, or throwing out a runner if he tried to reach for extra bases.

One summer I ran a good time in the sixty and a scout came up to talk to me about signing in the rookie league for the Royals if they had an opening for an outfielder, so here was my chance to play pro ball. I could tell how excited my dad was, even though he is always careful not to show too much emotion. It seemed like a chance for both of us somehow, something we could live out together, the same dazzling dream. But I knew even then it was mostly his vision, and whatever grains I had to offer toward it were already trickling out, my heart and desire beginning to wane at seventeen. My dad talked to me about switch-hitting, or maybe moving to second, because you don't see many five-foot-eight center fielders in the major leagues; he said this might be a good opportunity, but offers down the road were bound to come if I just worked hard enough and got tougher mentally. But they never did because I quit two years later. I didn't have the killer's instinct, a fatal weakness. I saw it in Wob, too, a gentle soul who loved the game but never played with that streak of special meanness any sport requires in order to be the very best.

My dad and I drove around Kansas City, talking about the possibilities; Florida was a world away, and looking back now there was no way I could have left my home and future wife to play somewhere in the sticks. I just didn't love it enough, which would become my secret heresy. I loved the love my dad had for my playing, the palpable and sweaty urgency of it, but maybe that's all I really cared about, what we shared together when the game ended. He didn't push me like other dads, but his love for sports quietly pervaded everything our family did and believed until few alternatives had room to grow, let alone be mentioned: competition was the mantra of his life, the reason he could leave his working-class roots on the poor side of a paper mill town in Michigan and make a better life for himself and his family, the one constant, abiding value we ate with our bread each night. There were only winners and losers, the strong and the weak, nothing in between, no mitigating shades of gray. I felt inarticulate and dumb in the face of my own accelerating trajectory, not just at home but everywhere I went because I believed somehow without actually experiencing it firsthand that there were other points of view outside the world of sports and competition, other kinds of people and values whose mere existence would cause a quickening in my blood and later change me, even if I had not yet met them.

What sports gave us more than anything (what it gives us still) is a common language hewn out of the efforts of athletes' bodies and our own on a playing field in the now or long ago, with its own built-in, unshakable grammar, and subjects never veering too far from crude, hard arithmetic (the W−L column, who made or didn't make the final shot). With language as simple yet as poetical as this, we could swap souls, move in each other's skin, embellish if we had to, make vivid once again an instant in time when a decision seemed to *matter* even if it was just a game, to define by its very outcome the character of a player and thus, by extension, of ourselves. To never give up, to be honest, to play through pain — what other verities could a man or woman possibly need? And they were all right there, codified by our own experiences and those of an entire nation. We could be passionate without dropping our guard, walking and talking the fine edge between real communication and shooting the shit. But often I have felt the beginning of tears well up in my eyes for no reason when we're talking about the Final Four, or a hitting streak, or the phantom hook of the Ali− Liston fight, and always wondered why.

So often, though, even as a kid, I suspected a terrible inad- equacy; sometimes I wanted to say, "Some things aren't a game," but I knew enough to keep my mouth shut. I would risk alienation or worse, bafflement and incomprehension, things I myself didn't understand. Instead I clung to some deep interior limb growing all the time and saw my inchoate belief confirmed everywhere I looked: my father was right, the world is indeed

divided between the winners and the losers, but the winning
and the losing often happens with a randomness that has
little to do with talent or volition. More troubling still was the
gnawing notion that it did not necessarily have anything to do
with drive or the competitive spirit but blind pig luck, a graze
of a ghostly fingertip that could set a life to spiraling or ascending. The game was rigged — or so complex and mysterious it
amounted to the same thing. In fact, in the ways that truly mattered, how people really lived their whole lives, winning and
losing had nothing to do with it: there was only a deepening
context enfolded into incomprehensibility, tendons and tissues
so fine you could almost hear them tearing into something else.

I sensed this as the deepest reality I knew, but I didn't have
the words. Some kids were crippled at school, and most were
not; a girl from Turkey was perpetually picked on because of
her scimitar nose, and two huge black boys named Miles and
Andre were beloved because they were the tokens of their race
in a Catholic school where almost everyone was white and
everyone wore uniforms. My older brother Bill's head found
the hard, unforgiving surfaces of concrete and stone and other
boys' fists until concussions became like a woozy friend to him,
seven, eight, nine times — who knows how many — as he would
say, wiping his bloody nose obsessively like a pint-size drunk,
"Don't tell Mom, don't tell Mom." I crawled under some bushes
one summer to watch a neighbor clean his pistol on his back
porch when he pointed the glistening barrel at me, smiled, and
pulled the trigger on an empty chamber. I made haste backward
on my shirtfront, scuttling out of there. I heard the locusts
scream from the top of our house at sundown one hot evening
when I was nine and believed it was the end of the world — and
it was the end of the world, as it always is the end of the
world at such twilit hours when you dread the same sleep that

will help you forget the immutable fact of all endings. These ambiguities bled into me like a slow-spreading dye until my blood seethed in it, coursing down the strangely lit corridors of experience to the warping and shifting of shapes: at some point unknown to me I passed an invisible divide and came out the other side, troubled and surprised at the complexity of the world and my own inability to control or predict it. The often crude dichotomy of sports sometimes does not allow room for such ambiguity, and maybe that is why so many love and need them, including me; but they rarely are able to reflect what goes on around and inside us, the mysteries of living and dying that break out of the void like waves, granting dispensation here, catastrophe somewhere else: but where the pattern is, no one can say for sure. There really wasn't anything else to compare this gut feeling to, but I couldn't compare it to sports.

My decision to quit baseball suddenly, inexplicably, for reasons I still do not completely know, continues to haunt me, like the dust I see rising from so many American roads. My dad supported me in my decision, but something quietly died between us, some unspoken and common ground of under-standing that we lived out and played. We lived our connection during long innings and doubleheaders, a father—son telepathy running a one-way circuit from his heartbeat to mine: it was a privileged rite of passage, and I turned away from it. For some, it is not a passage at all but a place to live, a destination clearly marked: Go there, it seems to promise, and you never have to grow up. My father and I have never been closer than that postgame drive, I in my muddy uniform, he commenting with calm and easy sagacity how the game could have gone, or how it did go, or how it could go in the future: "You need to get your hands away from your body a little more at the plate." I miss those Zenlike instructions and the way we shared so much that was coded into our very genes. He was one of the best teachers I ever had, and knew just what to say, how to praise and instruct at the same time. I lived for his praise, and for the praise of my coaches, for any man older than I who could take the measure of myself and hold it up to me.

I wonder if Wob ever felt that; I wonder if he, like my own father, loved the game so much in his own quiet way that nothing else could compare with it; I wonder if part of his suicide had something to do with the loss of playing baseball, of the myriad rituals and easy camaraderie associated with it, if life after it just got to be too monotonous or too real. I don't know, and speculations about the dead simplify and muddle the context of their passing. But I know Wob loved baseball, maybe too much for all his meekness, and maybe that would have been reason enough to want to live, if only he could have kept playing. The way he cleaned his spikes with a special screwdriver seemed evidence enough. But he had a faraway look in his eyes even then, looking away toward some bleak horizon only he could see. Or am I guilty of seeing in retrospect small glimpses of his own murderer?

Why did you do it, Wob?
Why did you pull the trigger?

If I could talk to you again, Bruce, I would ask you about baseball; I would ask you what you loved about it, if you thought maybe, just maybe, you could play at the next level. I would ask you in a roundabout way (neither of us would have a thing to lose) why you sought out the small pebbles of your home at short, why you inspected them like a fastidious gardener, collecting them, then casting them away with your glove. I would ask you about the American dream and where it began to fail you, and about those fireflies that lit up the trees near the train tracks behind left field, the loudspeaker blaring Eric Clapton, the long-legged and heart-stopping girls who shaded their eyes from the sun. I'd ask you about your favorite part of the season and tell you about a second baseman in high school whose name was Tommy Brown, killed on graduation night by a drunk driver, his body torn in half. We would converse of dusty things, Bruce, maybe even pick up a handful of it somewhere. By and by we might get to the subject of your death, but it would not be the point, just a bright white marker somewhere down the road. We might even go out for a beer, though I know neither of us drinks beer; I would try to tell you why I quit playing ball, how your kindness meant so much to me at the time, and how you were the one on that new and final team who seemed truly decent to me, even noble in a way. We would have all the time in the world to talk about these things, Bruce, and you wouldn't have to feel alone.

But the death of a shortstop, especially a suicide, is an event far out on the edge of the American psyche, so strange and almost shameful that I do not think most people would want to dwell on it; it's a betrayal even greater than mine, Bruce, I who turned my back on competitive sports when it was all laid out before me. I need to tell you that, Wob: you need to know how few of us can understand that kind of fear and despair, including me. It's like that plane going down; the story hits the paper, but no one has a clue about what it means. We were spiritual cousins the moment I quit and disappointed my dad and the moment you decided to end your life; we are tied at the same gnawing root, only I had the blessings to see other roots, other possibilities.

I think I know what winning and losing is now because of

your haunting infield memory; I think they are one and the same, a brief veil lifting, the ancient and irretrievable song that sings only of the now before us, and the promise that sometime, somewhere, in some other faraway place, the losers and the quitters will lift the winners from their graves.

Notes from the Konukevi

For a couple of months now I've been living on the side of a
mountain in Samsun, Turkey, at the konukevi (or guesthouse),
watching the city below materialize each morning out of the
dissolving mist that lifts with such slow-moving and ceremoni-
ous restraint it's like the trailing end of a drawn-out kiss from
the steep, tree-covered slopes around me. I think everything
should be revealed this way, a new soufflé, a lover's body, an
heirloom brought down from the attic. It's a daily disappear-
ance and reappearance act that never gets old, and I already
know its changing, ever-shifting view will henceforth always be
a part of me.

I'm sorely tempted to call it my mountain, at least my first
and foremost — not, I hope, because I wish to possess any part
of it but because of the way it continues to give Turkey to me as
a wide, panoramic offering that contains within it something
I can only call deliverance. Apparently, the mountain is still up
for grabs because no Turk seems to want to claim it or even give
it a name, which I find quietly hopeful and astonishing: there's
nothing around to suggest it has any special significance, no
flags, no signs, no placards of any kind. When I asked a Turkish
friend about its name once, he looked at me with a puzzled
expression and said, "It has no name."

As far as mountains go, it's as gentle as they come, rising
gradually from the Black Sea less than a mile away in a bosom

of generous earth before its rounded top disappears into the clouds, with nary a jagged cliff face of exposed rock to show for itself. This Turkish mountain is not particularly dramatic or awe-inspiring and is in fact downright humble: some people might claim it's not a mountain at all, or if it is, one so gradual and hangdog poor it deserves some lesser designation somewhere down the pecking order. But it's a mountain to me, and a dear one at that, growing dearer every day for the fog-laden views it gives me, and in so many different and subtle ways it defies easy explanation or any explanation at all. Because I'm strangely at home here on the side of this mountain at the konukevi, like a part of me has always been here somehow, which continues to surprise me for a number of reasons that do not — like the mountain itself — lend themselves easily to utterance.

The basic facts are that I came to Samsun at the invitation of a Turkish friend, to teach and give a series of weekly lectures at Ondokuz Mayis University, the first American to ever do so — but these hardly get to the heart of the matter: they only point in the broad, sweeping direction of Asia with no other continent in sight. It's true I wanted to get away during my first sabbatical (who wouldn't?) — not away from my wife or home in the woods of northern Michigan but from something else that's been dogging me for years like a constant, inner ache I can't get rid of. But here on this nameless Turkish mountain the ache has subsided considerably and sometimes even disappears for days at a time, only to flair up again at unexpected moments.

So living on the side of this mountain as I watch the city fade and come back with the daily calls of Ezan haunting the thinning air is the best salve for the ache I've ever known, as is the long walk each day up to my office, which is often at chin level with the clouds, better than drink or movies or another temporary escape I could resort to in order to try to appease the nagging symptoms of this same ache. I smoke my allotted one daily cigarette on the balcony of my room looking out on the shimmering lights of the city and the sea, and I know I'll never be this free or happy again, or as lonesome. These facts alone have been sufficient to put me in a more or less permanent meditative mood during my time in Turkey living and writing on the mountain, something that feels a little otherworldly as if I'm caught between lifetimes and states of being, which I very well could be.

I think I'm beginning to understand now why some writers have to leave America for extended periods of time, why there are expatriate hangouts all over the world, why some people feel the excruciating need to get away and stay away from everything they've ever known, which is no doubt related in no small way to my own peculiar and nagging ache. As a lifelong midwesterner, I haven't known much else — and so I had no way of knowing before coming here that the ache I don't fully understand is somehow part and parcel of the same lodestone of peculiarly American woe chipped from the enormous monolith of towering stone called the American dream or its rough-hewn equivalent, with hardly ever a chance for perspective-taking until I ended up here in Turkey. All I know for sure is that I'm aware of a slight difference and separation like layers of bright gossamer being pulled away, that who I am in Michigan and was in my native Nebraska is not quite who I am here.

And who is that exactly?

Who is the forty-one-year-old man living on the side of a mountain in Samsun at the mercy of his hosts and the kindness of Turkish strangers?

To tell the truth, I don't know: I only know that I'm a

stranger in this place, and have come to relish this outsider status for reasons beyond my immediate grasp, like some vast exhalation of relief that is still ongoing even as I look down on Samsun's glittering chandelier of city lights.

But two days ago I walked down the side of the mountain to the university's Olympic Center and was followed by a magnificent white dog that looked like an arctic wolf, the white dog trailing about ten yards behind me on the winding and overgrown brick path. I stopped a few times to look back at it, for I was warned that dogs run wild on this part of the mountain and in fact all over Turkey. The white dog looked wild all right, lean and hungry-looking, with a snout like the stock of a polished Winchester. Each time I stopped the white dog stopped also, like we were in lockstep together in our mutual pause-and-go that punctuated our descent. I was sure we would part company at the bottom for the busy highway I had to cross, so when I got there I took one last look at the white dog, who still maintained its ten yards' distance, only this time with one of its front paws raised as if to ask me a final question before we left each other for good, and then I crossed the highway.

I had no way of knowing that the ache was coming back, but my brief encounter with the dog that was really no encounter at all served to somehow make me wonder, in a brief but delirious bout of disorientation, where and who I was and what I was doing at the northern end of Turkey. In the starkest and simplest terms, you get on a plane and leave: that's what it always comes down to. The destination doesn't even matter all that much, as long as it's somewhere else far away. Maybe I even believed I could leave the ache behind, drop it like a bad habit and become someone entirely new and fresh unto the world, which has even happened here at least for a little while.

But slowly I've come to realize that not even this beloved

mountain can get rid of the ache for good, that it's somehow managed to track me down because I carried it inside all along with its peek-a-boo shutters and symptoms popping up again no matter where I go, as the ache is lodged so deeply inside me I'm convinced only death could finally rid me of it. Because an hour or so later, coming back from the gym, I saw the white dog stretched out and freshly killed on the same highway where we had last looked each other in the eyes. I could see it about a quarter of a mile away, about thirty feet from the littered shoulder, the filaments of its fur lifting in the wind and shining like white fire. I went up to the white dog and discovered that she was female and saw how only her face was smashed while the rest of her lean body looked perfectly intact, perfect in every part and lineament of rib and tendon so that I couldn't help crying — crying for the white dog and crying for myself and a thousand other things, crying because I had unwittingly led her to her death and because she was a white, wild, and beautiful dog that never had a chance.

I grabbed her by all four paws and dragged her off the highway, the pads of her feet still warm, though it could have been from the heat of the concrete in the sun. You touch a dead white dog like this and somehow it's like touching the map and meaning of the world no one understands, which you are still an indisputable if infinitesimal part of, a map that goes on and on between the dead and the living and the sky above the Black Sea beside a crumbling, falling-down sidewalk in Samsun, Turkey. The death of the dog was something I couldn't share with anyone, as our happenstance and fatal meeting took place under the auspices of chance and isolation far beyond the province of understanding. Besides, whom would I tell it to anyway in my nearly nonexistent and nascent Turkish? The truth was, I had been afraid of the dog when I first saw her, but I also couldn't help but admire her beauty and the way she followed me down the mountain like a four-legged animate candle of white flames, an angel perhaps taking the form of a dog or even a dervish who had come to show me something I had never seen before.

Later I realized that the dog was connected to the ache that continues to swim in the bloodstream of my veins, the ache that must in the final analysis be God-charged and insatiable, connected to every living thing and to the life force itself, caught up in the infinite sorrow that somehow attends to each of us. I had thought, for instance (and this is where time and chronology collapse and the cards of a life are radically reshuffled), that I had left the overwhelming Nebraska sky of my childhood long behind, the kind of sky no sane person would ever want to face, a sky that simply obliterates every comfort and consolation there is, in service of an impossible truth, that we are all somehow free-falling through every moment of our lives, even as we walk down a street, that an eternity of space surrounds us on every side which we can do nothing about except recognize it once in a while in order to try to get it out of our minds. I thought I had left such void episodes back in Omaha, only to find that the void was back in the sky above the Black Sea while I knelt down before the white dog that had been killed trying to follow me.

Could or should I tell anyone about the white dog and my time on the mountain?

Could I dare to mention the ache and do justice to its glowing debris trail of symptoms and signs?

The answer is yes and no, never and always: the answer isn't even for me to say. But now I think that the ache must be like a spark in the lining of my heart or a worm unable to find lasting sustenance in anything it burrows into, that it's a slow burning through my innards toward the conflagration of my life — though even these foolhardy stabs at metaphor in no way really describe it. But the white dog was looking walleyed at the road and the sky, at me, at the astonishment of her last moments before the truck or car hit her and went on — she was looking past the sea into the ink of the stars and beyond them into the vastness of nothing and all that nothing contains. I didn't close her eyes. I didn't touch her again. But I knew I would never forget her, that her wild and roaming nature was somehow congruent with something inside me, that we were, at least for a moment, curious about each other and almost friendly.

I made sure her body lay well off to the side of the highway in a comfortable position, though of course she was beyond comfort in a place that rattles like a Styrofoam cup caught in a chain-link fence. I walked across the highway, not wanting to look at any driver's face for fear of self-betrayal, back to the foot of the mountain that continues to show me things I know I'll always cherish until the day I myself lay dying, when I will see it again in its shifting white meringue of fog in the intimacy of an overwhelming truth that cannot be articulated, only embodied.

2

Folk Music

Beggar on the Danube

On Béla Bartók Street in Budapest, you can see a dapper blind
man pointing with his tapered white cane, feeling for obstacles
and doorways, like a Richter needle registering slight tremors
a few inches above the ground. You can see a crippled beggar
on Szabadsag Bridge with his orthopedic stick, his hand held
out in front of his body like a small baptismal font, brown and
deeply creased; you can see an old woman sitting out in front
of the Central Market on Vamhaz Korut, holding her hands out
for money, then folding them together in prayer when someone
gives her a coin. The rims of her fingernails are made of soot
and grime so deep they must have penetrated the cuticles like
dye made of engine oil, never to be washed away, never to be
forgotten. They fit around her nails like tiny aureoles of doom
as if they had been painted on by a scavenging angel. I think
they are the color of volcanic ash, and that someday a beautiful
flower will grow out of them.

I dream of hands like these. They make their way out of the
darkness without faces or bodies, like slow-moving snakes,
hands that materialize out of the black ink of consciousness
and conscience. They move toward my face like spiders, they
want to touch my forehead, my ears, the bridge of my nose,
to feel the contours of my eye sockets. They are filthy, ravaged
hands, deformed and mangled, missing a knuckle or a finger
here and there, scarred, battered, bruised, and broken. What

69

do they want with a troubled dreamer? The question is always asked with outrage — and now I think it's they who should be outraged, they who should have the right to ask, *How can you ignore me?* But I am helpless in the dream, my own hands pinned behind my back so that these other hands can explore my face and body however they want.

Will they hit me? Will they break my nose? Will they reach lower to touch me, to arouse me or to hurt me? Is the beggar on the Danube free to touch me while I cannot even push his hands away? Are they the wings of an angel coming to claim me? These hands enrage me, they appall me, they ask without words for some change, a cigarette, a bottle of beer; and now they are free to do what they wish, to touch me however they want, to hurt me, to tease me, to mock me. The hands are black and white and all shades of color, red, yellow, and mottled with age, tattooed and zebra-striped; they are the hands of God and the hands of a runaway teenager, always reaching out to me, always coming forward, moving like wisps of smoke or cold marble to the threshold of contact. But in the dream, they never take advantage of my helplessness; they never hurt me or tease or shame me. They reach out with infinite care, so slowly and delicately it's almost like they are reaching to remove a rose petal from my hair. They move to touch me, to caress me, to love me, and to heal me, never to harm me. And this is where the dream becomes my grief, for as the hands touch me in this way, the fear and the mistrust inside me dissolve like salt in water and I feel the pity in their fingers, the pity that they know and the pity that I have so often ignored, the pity they are communicating to me through the ends of their fingertips.

Surely the hands of the beggar on the Danube are among the strangest, most troubling sights in the universe; surely they indicate that good and evil are not so simple, that no one is

exonerated from the touch of another and the teetering scale
that hangs in the balance. I have seen these hands in every big
city, in alleys and street corners and doorways on busy boule-
vards; I have seen them trying to shade eyes from the sun, to
stem the flow of commerce, and to bridge the gaping distance
between the haves and the have-nots. I have seen them light
cigarettes and blow noses, rock faces back and forth in laughing and sobbing, search for a pebble at the bottom of a shoe.
They reach without touching, because that is all that they have
the power to do. These hands pray the way Jesus prayed in the
garden, the way a child lifts a paper airplane to the sun, the way
a bird raises its wings in flight or takeoff, the way a nurse or
caretaker removes a piece of bloody gauze or a mother changes
a dirty diaper. They are familiar with the muck and the mire, the
crude matter of the gutter, shit and afterbirth, coinage, ejacu-
late, rotting garbage from a dumpster. They touch the painful
nerves of this world and never stop feeling.

The rest of us keep our hands to ourselves; I myself wash my
hands several times a day. Few reach out to perfect strangers,
until, perhaps, we become strangers ourselves. Even the dapper
blind man and his white cane is looking for something with
this extension of his hand, feeling his way ahead for shapes
and textures that he can make sense of. The world is a sloping grid to him, a series of undulating ripples with surprises
at every corner, synapses firing in his central nervous system
through touch and the possibility of touch: he could be one of
the few people whose every move is an anticipation of touch
both realized and nearly missed, touch that beckons him forward and touch that makes him stop.

Like the beggar on the Danube and the beggar at the market,
the blind man knows something that most of us have forgotten, that for the world to have any meaning or hope, we must

reach out to one another, though our reaching out may be rebuffed or ignored; we must hold our palms up to the sun in front of strangers to see if they will touch us back, to find if they will give not only of their change but also of their kindness, the graze of their fingertips, to hold and to heal. Is anything more revolutionary than this, that we could hold our hands out for strangers to touch? If we, like the blind man, did not have sight, would we then know how to avoid the beggars — or would we bump into them so that we would be surprised at the contact?

One day I know I will see the beggar on the Danube in the middle of the Szabadsag Bridge, that we have, in a sense, an appointment. Each day I have crossed this bridge to get to Pest; I know that he will be at the halfway point of the bridge, that I can see him from the hills of Buda, hunched over and reaching out. Today is the secret day I have chosen to hold his hand longer than it takes to drop a few forints into it. I want to see, touch, and witness this hand for myself, and in doing so, I know that for whatever reason, I will learn to cherish this exchange as a precious gift. As I approach the bridge, I start to get nervous, feel that fate has led me here, that I am supposed to understand this encounter somehow and tell myself again and again what I think it means. The beggar has been coming back to me at odd moments, when I turn a street corner, sip a cappuccino, scribble a few lines in my journal. He seems present somehow everywhere, on the shifting light between buildings and the sudden scattering of pigeons. He is somehow in the polished windows of fashionable boutiques and the green oxidized hues of statuary around the city; in fact, there is nowhere he does not go or suddenly appear, as much a part of this place and its history as the woman holding the palm leaf at the top of Gellert Hill.

Today is the day I will hold the beggar's hand. Can you understand what a big deal this is, how it adds up to a small moment of hope in a world out of whack? As we cross Béla Bartók Street, I can already see him at his post halfway across. I am holding Tina's hand. My heart starts to beat faster. No one knows about my secret plan, not even my beloved who is at my side. We are moving at the speed of the river, maybe faster. The beggar sees me from one hundred feet away. He has seen me before. I can hardly meet his eyes. As we near him, he shuffles a few feet in our direction and I take a few forints out of my pocket; I go straight for his hand, stare at it and memorize it as best as I can. When we reach the beggar I drop the few coins into the palm of his hand and let my own hand stay there for an instant longer: his hand is brown and soft, yielding, like an oven mitt just out of the heat. His hand is surprisingly soft, not nearly as hard as it looks, soft the way warm dirt is soft, coming out of the earth to be crushed or fired in an urn. I am quietly thankful and bashful to make contact, to feel at least his first few fingers and the outside of his hand. The whole thing happens in less than five seconds, but I know I will never forget those five seconds or the way his hand felt.

On the north side of the river, something is sparkling in the water, a blinding and dazzling jangle of light, like a spinning prism held up to the sun. Where did it come from? Tina and I both see it, this dancing star in the water, this beautiful and shining thing. Then it is gone; it disappears into the river or the air above the water. We look at each other. Did you see that? Did you see the sparkling thing in the water? The city doles out this brief mystery on a whim, a mystery like a benediction, a mystery whose timing might have nothing or everything to do with the beggar on the Danube. I choose to believe it has everything to do with the beggar, the beggar who is everyone's brother and son, father and friend, whether we choose to think it is so or not. The deep grooves of his hands, those warm, soft mitts, prove the connection. Then, before we know it, we're on the other side of the river.

Looking for the Bishop

Looking for the bishop, I thought I almost saw him in the alpenglow of a harvest moon, in a hedge bursting with buds no bigger than a child's fingerprints, in a neighbor's plastic pinwheel spinning clockwise in the wind. I thought I saw him in tiny grains of hope, in a woman brushing the hair from a sullen boy's face, in the balm of sudden healing from shredded clouds racing from the stars. The bishop is will-o'-the-wisp, a puff of breeze, more hopeful in his flowing red gown than any figure I know. He walks by my window on his daily sojourns, emerging from the hidden chambers of peace and clarity to sustain me in surprising ways, a figure so out of character with this part of central Michigan as to be laughable, lovable, and mysterious all at once. His hood shrouds his head like an oddly draped flower, announcing his presence before you notice the thin, small body sheathed in flowing folds. I have never seen his hair. The bishop is East Indian, with a triton beard and long, delicate fingers that taper off like the hands in a Byzantine painting. He is doubly, triply strange for all that, a man visiting from another world yet a part of this one, more vivid because of this. No one can quite tell me how he has come to be here, but would any reason make his presence less mysterious?

I see him walking everywhere in this small town, taking the night air upon an evening, the hems of his robe swirling in gentle eddies around his slippered feet. A part of me wants to

follow him or fit inside one of his pockets like a bright polished
key. I would take up residence in his flowering hood, become
his watchtower, his bird's-eye view, or hunker down where the
clean folds of his robe billow out into forgetfulness, the ripple
of a fresh, gentle wind. I want to walk the way he does, watchful and alert, more incongruent here than a rare plumaged bird
whose colors remain unbesmirched by the drabness of winter.
He is the cardinal bird that could make all the difference, burning his sacred red feathers in a slow fire that will never die out.
He walks by my house sometimes, and each time my heart gets
a little lighter and clearer, opening a tiny door that feels like
a frail hope ascending until I realize I am supposed to notice
him, take his example to heart, follow his lead, and become
pure, vivid color in a land of black and white.

What do I know about him? Nothing I don't see in his
thoughtful gait, in the alert owl look in his dark brown eyes.
Nothing he does not already show me, though he does not
know it, in a simple long walk, the veil of a consciousness
he gives me each time I see him. I need his walk like a covert
response to things that make me uneasy, to the vague malaise
dripping like a bad faucet at the heart of town, the malice of
revved-up pickup trucks with gun racks; the bishop shows me
how to live here in subtle, surprising ways, how to walk in a
small town, with the kind of grace I ached for without realizing
it, seeing his long red robe and careful steps over patches of ice.

You could go a long time without an example like the
bishop — twenty, thirty years, a whole life. You could ignore
people or signs like him, not take them into your heart or let
them peel it open layer by precious layer. You could choose to
close the curtains or drapes, lock the door and turn up the TV,
but if the bishop should ever walk by your window or down
your neighborhood street, you could have the opportunity

to sense the hushed lightness trailing behind him, the seed
blossoms of his robes riding the air to find a place to plant
themselves and take up growing. You could work the bishop
walking by into any belief system you have, into the words of a
prayer undirected to any god, into a chant for hope and brightness, a candle flame flickering in your cupped hands. You could
use the bishop however you like, to get over sadness or death,
or loneliness that drops like a single stone into a dark well, to
imagine your life past the threshold where you are who you
have always intended to be, that upright person in the mirror
without longing or shame. But you must be careful with him,
handle him as you would a porcelain jar that contains all the
secret and dangerous ingredients of spring, or the fragrance of
a night you do not want to forget. His presence is careful and
oh-so-delicate, because he comes sparingly and when you least
expect it, like all good surprises.

I hear his name mentioned sometimes around the Alma
campus: the bishop is leaving for Brazil, the bishop is going
back to India for a spell, the bishop is flying to New York.
Sometimes he sits by himself in the faculty dining area, arrayed
in his exotic uniform, serene and staring out the window. I've
seen him eat hard-boiled eggs as if the earth's ovals were at
home in his mouth, a beneficent and cosmic gape. I don't particularly want to know the minutiae of his life, the name of his
native village, his conversion to the Orthodox Church long ago,
the demands of his office. I smile when I see him and he smiles
back, we chat about the weather and the courses he teaches.
Maybe sometime we will go into things more deeply, but it
doesn't seem to matter much. What's important is that he's
here, that I have the chance to see him. He need not even know
how important he has become. Maybe someday I will tell him
how much his odd presence means to me, how it has gained

its own quiet and hopeful momentum, that I was hardly aware of it myself before this, that his walking is simple grace and nothing more. Does he need to know this now or ever? Would it violate a pact no one can see or understand?

Stranger, we have met and touched briefly in a land far away from home, and the brief exchanges have sustained me. The unknown distance between us spools out into the infinite, and we fill it with hope like bright, clear water dripping from the eaves. You are not of this place; I am not of this place. Together and separately, we part the invisible waters of our destinies and notice how a bird alights on a slender branch. We are far away from home. We have forgotten what home is. You travel to every corner of the earth and the taste and memory of it all reel by in a kaleidoscope of human touches and voices, with people reaching out to you, and I know this same kind of ministry happens right here, right now, adding to the same continuum where nothing is lost and everything merges into one.

Seeing you disappear down the street or around the corner does not frighten me; death itself after you have departed does not frighten me. I have nothing to run from in your presence. After you leave and pick up your mail, the ache throbbing in me since I first knew consciousness subsides a little, becomes bearable, becomes my dear friend. I believe in the invisible when I see you, I believe in the unseen net that catches me everywhere I go, the same frail net held up by threadbare strings so few and precious and strong that I dare not dwell on them for long. You remind me, Bishop, that I could be catapulted from this very chair right now to another part of the world by catastrophe or loss, that I could lose everything in fire or flood, that I some-day will lose it all anyway, the ring of laughter, the memory of love in strange rooms, that the people I care about will leave me behind, that I will leave them knowingly and unknowingly, that I will only see many of them just four or five times more, that what's put in motion cannot be stopped, must be played out, that I, like you, will continue this strange wandering for the rest of my life, that I'm finally ready for this, at least on my good days, that I can never quite trust human permanence again, that that's how it is, a mystery, a slow-moving prayer. Maybe you have known this all along. Maybe it is only this you have intended to show me. But intentional or not, more and more each day I wake with a sense of wonder, telling myself and believing that anything is possible today, good and bad, that I will notice both and try my best to love them in their open or secret surprise.

I used to think human intimacy was a matter of deep disclosures, physical contact, constant presence; but I no longer believe this. Now I think it can happen anytime, anywhere, in seeing a brightly robed bishop from another part of the world taking a stroll, hands folded behind his back, noting the beauty around him. I need hope incarnate like him, I need to glimpse his example more than once in a while. I need to fall in lockstep behind him, not because he is Christian or a bishop but because he changes the molecules of the air into something reverent, mysterious, and faintly humorous, as if God himself truly is playing a joke on us, not a knee-slapper but some kind of gentle benediction that gives us the capacity to smile. I greet him when I see him, and he is always pleased and surprised, and I am always pleased and surprised. Wonder works this way, in sudden, inexplicable meetings. Hello, Bishop, hello. Each time I see you I greet you without words, thankful that you are here, thankful that I'll always have your example in the back of my mind, that grace never disappears, that it's subtle and clean like washed sheets on a line, that it lives in the manifold openings and unfoldings of things coming to life and curving themselves to the sun. I need you more than I can say, but now I know it is not you yourself I need really, but something inside you that beckons me to follow. Hello, Bishop. If I never see you again, I will continue to look for you anyway in anything that is vivid and real, in darting sparrows, in broken glass, in the people I come across who wail and laugh and cry without opening their mouths.

Doctor Whisper

Today I will pick up an old man from the hospital, a man who has lived alone his whole life and whose house is littered with dirty dishes, spiritual manuals, and academic journals from 1962. A wooden crucifix hangs in his living room like a whalebone salvaged from the sea, and there's no apparent correlation between the piled debris of his house and the odd purity of his mind, which tries to recall every date and every encounter he has ever had, mumbling it like a vast, buzzing hive of invisible bees that swarms a constant murmur inside his head, pages of untranslated Greek and dialogues between people you have never heard of, voices coming out of the ceiling and the walls from thirty years ago, and his own voice speaking under all of them like the hum coming off a vibrating glass rim, telling you where the batteries are in case you forgot and the secret list of every hand he has ever touched, along with receipts from the dentist, old records of Respighi, and journal entries pertaining to the death of a childhood pet.

The truth is, he has been speaking like this for years, for decades, all of his adult life, building bridges out of the roof of his sputtering mouth to welcome any and all comers. He says what he says in a perpetual stream often barely above a whisper, eschewing causation or even context, as if you are inside his head like a friendly tumor, and you think to yourself, *No one talks like this*, but here he is, the troubled glossolalia of all your childhood dreams, voices coming out of the cavern of his throat, and he's trying to tell you all about it, leaving nothing out, eyeball to eyeball, trying to communicate the one essential thing, to broach the distance between himself and you so that it remains hushed and intimate forever, to hold you in a word and make you love him once and for all, the radio waves of his incessant love coming into your ears in the frequency of static or the chamber music of Brahms. He's like a one-man station sending out signals all across the world to no one in particular, bulletins about the weather on this day in 1955, God's children and a recipe for cider, a banjo player fiddling in the corner, racial injustice, awe training, the pain in his neck that won't go away, what he ate for breakfast and how it moved through his body like a boa constrictor, how Christ spoke to him once in a radiant star that lodged beneath his tongue in semaphores of reckoning, the way sex would explode him out of his body like a cannon shot of confetti or how his aunt told him of a dream where she woke up in bed with Joe Louis.

It's all there in his glistening mouth, the ghost of his father hair-triggered in rage, the cardboard shoes he made while working at the A&P, his doctoral work at the University of Michigan. He leaves nothing out in his hushed speech, assuming you will always listen and understand no matter what he tells you, a one-way exchange of great personal significance that you will one day cherish for reasons you will never understand. He believes everything he says, and he wants you to believe it too; he is telling you this again and again, sometimes calmly, sometimes raising his voice barely above a quaver, but always, ultimately, in a whisper you can't quite make out, like a cryptic stone door opening in mystery, his lips hardly moving across tiny lakes of spittle.

Not enough to say he's old or lost it, that he's a walking

parody of himself and the lovable pariah everyone seeks to avoid but can't stop thinking about. Not enough that he would follow you around all day on an invisible leash just to tell you what he knows and has seen, that it really did matter that he couldn't change a flat tire in front of his father without fumbling with the iron, that he broadcasts messages via e-mail entitled "My Whereabouts" to people who do not know him or hardly care, that he ingratiates himself into every conversation and cannot stop talking, that he has food stains on his shirt and smells like furniture polish, a living cautionary tale of what no one wants to become, a mateless old man of doubtful sexuality who has given his entire life to a college that has moved on without him, tapping the wristwatch with his alma mater etched across it from time to time to make sure it is still working. None of that explains who and what he really is, except as a hint that he's the carrier of an impossible, maddening love that risks ridicule and mockery simply in order to be. Sometimes he speaks in jewels of pure aphorism anyway, which come off his tongue like radiant fish to find you surprised at your own sudden and overwhelming affection. But he is always talking and will always speak, even unto the grave, his words spooling out into the great beyond to find us one day threadbare and abandoned at some strange interval when the realization hits that somehow his lonely, babbling life contained something essential and is coming back, immutable, clearer than other human speech.

Today I will pick him up from the hospital after a procedure he has been uncharacteristically afraid to talk about. I am dreading it, not because I feel put out or hassled, but because slowly, inexplicably, and very, very softly, like one of his own whispers that carries across the space between us in a puff of breeze-blown cottonwood seed, I have discovered how beautiful he really is. I have found myself thinking of him suddenly with such tenderness and concern that it makes me want to get on my hands and knees and ask forgiveness for a wrong I did not even know I had committed, a wrong I know in my heart I will commit again and again whenever I take him for granted. Already he haunts me and he is not even gone. Is this what he's been trying to communicate this whole time? Is this the overwhelming truth that runs like a current of murky water under all of his whispers? What am I to do with these contradictions, these real-life stresses, this old man who won't leave me alone when I see him or when I am looking at the ingredients on a can of soup in the grocery store? Every way I turn and squirm, every time I try to get away from him, dismiss him somehow, the same answer comes back to me in the form of his own quiet voice newly restored: just love him, just do that simple, astonishing thing.

What if some terrible information is revealed to him and I alone am there to see and hear his sobs and quakes? What will I, could I, say or do then? Suddenly this odd old man called Dr. Whisper has decided to make me his brief caretaker and he has become vivid and real to me, a figure not to make fun of but to cherish beyond all reckoning. Suddenly he has been trans-formed from a lovable old bachelor to a kind of holy man, one who gave his whole life to a profession, whose true gift resides in the sheer enormity of his reaching out to everyone he meets. He's speaking even now to be heard, remembering everything you ever told him, every lunch and meeting, every word that bends and falls off your tongue like a piece of ripe fruit. He is like haunting itself, looking, searching, seeking for someone, anyone, to talk to.

If you saw him coming down the walk half a block away you would already know that he is preparing to speak to you and you will not understand a word he says, but he will still communicate something heartbreaking and essential; what it means and why he chose you is something yet to be revealed until the day comes when you cup your ears to his mouth and find it closed forever.

Starlight in a Spoon

I see my mother at the window over the sink in a cathedral
of pale light, timeless, eternal, held in a moment rinsing the
dishes with wisps of stray hair lifting at her temples like spider
legs. I see her as God or an angel must see her, a little haggard,
frail as porcelain, tiredly beautiful. She is worn out and reflec-
tive, her hair moving like brushstrokes or waves so fine they
ripple with a seismic vibration deep inside the earth. I want to
see her like this again and to wash away the deep melancholy
riding in the crests of her face, pulling with a tidal gravity all
that she is doubting and accepting in doubt, to take those
wisps of hair and place them in a book where she fits between
words of praise that take her back to her beloved lakes in northern Michigan where she was a girl and knew clean blue water
on a still bright day. She's far off in her aloneness, and there's
no way to reach her or communicate this crucial fact, a world so
deep and lost and true that no one could ever reach her except
one of her own children crying out.

Like God looking through a boy's eyes, I suddenly see why
people create art, why men kill, and why none of it, the sublime
or the terrible, could ever touch the eternity of one woman's
face as she is washing the dishes. I have seen it all before, the
hands that hold the dishes, and the knowledge that I saw her
somehow outside time, vivid and exposed under the aspects of
eternity. The moment chooses me to show her this way, electing

itself out of the many thousands, to take me down the long passageway where choice cannot go, the neurons and chemicals in my brain turning and swirling only for this, to be used up for a truth that leaves every synapse behind. I wait to be summoned like this every day without knowing it and suddenly here she is, larger than a dream. We go through it again, the folly of growing up and the strange epiphanies it brings like images in a handheld kaleidoscope, she as a young mother and I as the starstruck watcher on the edge of my life who could lose it at the crucial moment of revelation. I want to lose it this way, if I can see her or anyone for who they really are, a ghost ride into the caverns of time where they slope and split and fall away in empty husks.

My father doesn't make it into this scene; he's gone like a rumor to the legends of work. He'll show up in other places and times of their own choosing, but not here. Instead it's just the two of us in the old house, and I'm on the other side of clarity, not the clarity hinged by any aureole of memory, but the distinct and brilliant curves of a moment liberated from time to move by itself above the rising steam and pale light that wash over her face. It's true that longing has brought me here, but that longing is like a booster that does its work and is jettisoned as soon as the rocket reaches outer space: I notice less the quality of rays that turn her into a body of light than I become a part of them, her skin so white and nearly translucent that she rises up into a prayer as the mask of her face falls away. Keep going, Mom, I whisper to myself; keep going; don't ever stop. An arctic light surrounds her, not in glowing ice but in piercing clarity; no one will ever wash dishes this way again, no one will ever fall into the clouds of this water like a shape finding itself in curves, in the apples of her breasts and in her shoulders leaning over the sink; she is already passing from one phase of life to another in front of my eyes and I sense the transition, like a tragic awakening. The space between us grows larger and more distinct, an ever-expanding map, and there's no way to shorten this distance because distance itself is the criterion of my love, to preserve this separation and to honor it, knowing it can't be any other way.

Now I realize I have wanted to write about this one moment for a long time, maybe my whole life, without even knowing it, because only it can show me everything I have to lose and everything I have to gain, the human stakes of this human life, how chronology fails the moment I try to put things into sequence. I have wanted to write about her at the window washing dishes because it contains both closeness and distance, like an interior fugue that chases its own tail to arrive at a complete stillness, because of the floating, iridescent bubbles that mimic the radiance of the sun, a young woman washing the dishes, a grace that shatters time and space. She has nothing to do with me and yet she is everything, my whole world and compass, the difficult water I have tried to breathe. Then I left the world of stories, not believing in anything that couldn't break out of its skin into pure light, like my own mother who threatened me with her own transcendence; she was the story, the soap bubbles, her soft auburn hair, how I could not, did not, exist for her at that moment and how there is a perfect accuracy in this, coming out of my life like a whispered chant. By being fully absorbed in washing the dishes and thinking her own private thoughts, a necessary part of me died; and this death was quick and shocking, full of strange forebodings. She became a stranger to me in that instant, and I have never recovered.

She is going, she is almost gone, sucked like a thread of smoke through a needle's eye, a living haunt with hands like someone out of an Edvard Munch painting, strangely angelic and noodle-thin, halfway between substantiality and a cloud, a ghost made of skin whose eyes peal back the window-light of eternity. I stood perfectly still on the axis of a spinning world, so that I swear the kitchen revolved around us like a slow-moving carousel and God came down in the form of that light and started to consume her in his love, my love, celebrating her in the starlight of a spoon that came through the overcast sky that day long ago in October. She can't let me follow because she doesn't even realize I'm there, which is another kind of dying. Light touches the dishes and lands on the counter and on her alabaster arms, immersing her in a water so deep I can't dive in and swim after her. I can't follow; I can't close the gap that separates us, can't tell her what it means. All I know is that she will go back some day to the source of this watery light, and I'll still be here on the other side, hearing the soft clink of the dishes, watching the unbearable lilt of her delicate hair rise and fall without a sound in the light coming through the kitchen window.

A Prejudice of Teeth

They less shine than carry their own dull, crooked light like so many unlit candles that keep opening bite-sized doorways to Turkey and to Asia each time I see them. I've had to keep myself from staring and yipping out loud like eurekas gone awry whenever I find myself peering into their mouths, for I need to remember that a smile from anyone anywhere is a gift and a sunrise of inestimable value, which I'm on high alert to remind myself of.

Nevertheless, I've become a secret chronicler and collector of ramshackle grins macabre, a voyeur of tea-stained incisors and sampler of crumbling eyeteeth, the more mangled and snaggle-toothed the better, like some demented miner or archeologist intent on slowly making his way through the stalactite caverns of other people's mouths, one by chomping one, hoping to come upon the hull of a gleaming arc that will finally reveal some painful but necessary truth once and for all. I never pegged myself as such, nor thought I'd come to notice or care so keenly about the teeth of other people and an entire nation, some of them so rubble worn it looks as though they've been chewing their way through blackened seaweed or dining on coal dust for years.

For since I've come to Turkey I've been taking a private census of people's mouths, drilling into them with an invisible but penetrating flashlight strapped to my forehead, seeking

to confirm some long-undisclosed but disturbing truth about
certain biases and proclivities as hinted at by the snapshot
views of the retreating gumlines I see each day, for how we view
other people's teeth may very well tap into a whole undertow of
pride and prejudice that prevails between nations and different
parts of the world whose unfortunate but natural consequences
may be distrust and misunderstanding or even worse. I'm also
coming to learn that such madcap fascination and almost relish
can quickly teeter into condemnation and outright disgust
in alignment with this same shameful propensity, that it says
far more about me for instance and my cultural conditioning
than it could ever say about anyone's teeth in Turkey, that I've
been lit up and blindsided by too many rife images of a smiling
Christie Brinkley and all her sun-kissed kind sprawled over the
billboards, newsstands, and screens of America like so many
pillared rays shining down from above in a glittering Neverland
I implicitly mistook for the real thing.

Because who wouldn't want a smile like hers or Tom Cruise's?
Who wouldn't be willing to sacrifice a great deal for a plumb-
line straight and whitened row of perfect teeth? But with every
creaking coffin lid of a poor Turkish mouth I'm slowly coming
to realize I've been hoodwinked and led along an alabaster
path white as Ahab's whale, that for all my largely unexamined
beliefs in liberty and egalitarianism, it all boils down to whiteness somehow, that I have in fact cleaved and clung to such
shards and examples of this dazzling whiteness wherever I
could find them, mistaking them less for symbols or metaphors
than for the just deserts of a progressive and leading democ-
racy. There's bias and prejudice galore in this view of teeth, and
I can't deny it anymore. And this is more than passing strange
and fairly bizarre to consider as I go on actively courting the
wrecking-ball aftermath of so many Turkish mouths on buses,

sidewalks, or wherever else I may snatch a snapshot glimpse of them around the city of Samsun on the Black Sea, which can only confirm that I've been a longtime and witless member of the widespread American cult of flawlessness with its legions of corrective measures that make such dark and forbidding mouths almost inconceivable: that for all my professed skepticism toward unchecked free markets and advertising run amok in the pursuit of the almighty dollar that they have in fact done a number on me and claimed a good chunk of my soul, chewing away at with it with their minion termites like so many devouring seedlings glowing in the sun.

For I can't keep feeling a certain shiver of horror and pity along with what can only be described as the faint traces of a trailing superiority whenever I see such a set of rotting teeth: my teeth are not like theirs, I think but do not say, which has to be among the most shameful admissions of my life, however unspoken. I'm guilty of a sweeping oral indictment, a fixation that puts me squarely in the klieg light of a blinding American bias I've somehow come to internalize. And important questions necessarily follow from this, a little less shocking perhaps but still unsettling, that might even come simply out of simple ignorance and naïveté, or a kind of dubious cultural innocence: How did their teeth get to be so bad? Is it because so many don't have access to dental care or can't afford it?

But these questions hardly scratch the surface, for even as I bring this implicit judgment to many of the mouths I see each day, I can't help wanting to see more and more of them and somehow record or mark the most ravaged and neglected of these, to go down into these same mouths in order to reclaim a deeper kind of humanity that I've somehow lost during the years of my formation and that — who knows — was perhaps one of my main reasons for venturing this far abroad in this quasi-self-imposed exile. Because at the same time that I find many of these teeth shocking and nearly beyond recognition, I'm also coming to somehow love and even admire them, finding in their open and unabashed decay and ruin something of poignant, inestimable value that is quickly fading from my own country, the stark and unvarnished vulnerability before the relentless forces of time and chance and the inability or non-desire to do anything about them. For to live with and carry such sepia fog within one's very mouth must surely bespeak a certain kind of acceptance and perhaps even wisdom that's quickly fading if not nearly completely gone in the West, a dis-regard for oral vanity and the high-wattage gleam of what can only be finally construed as a dazzling and colossal falsehood.

I admit that being a furtive cliff diver of other people's mouths is a disturbing occupation, that it belies a vague unease that may indicate other as-yet undiscovered symptoms of a larger malaise. But I'm coming to think this mouth-brooding is important and needs to be done, wherever it may lead, if only to come to some new and fresh understanding, however flawed and imperfect, of what underwrites these pervasive and unset-tling views: the American gospel of bright perfection must be reckoned with somehow some way, as I have an inkling some-thing of profound importance is at stake. This same obsession hits very close to home, for my own dad's family have long been marked by bad, neglected teeth, in keeping with their poor and struggling background and nearly catastrophic distrust of doctors and dentists: even now I have a long-lost uncle whose teeth would rival any decaying set I've yet seen in Turkey or anywhere else, a mouth that tugs and tugs at me in ways that almost bring me to my knees.

Because how can you correct where you come from and what you are?

Why should you even want to?

This is where these crumbling Turkish teeth keep leading me, pulling me along bit by pockmarked bit. They keep reminding me that perfection is not possible, and that maybe there's something even a little sinister in the very idea of a total whitewash, that we as human beings are stained and meant to fall apart eventually, that this is part of our burden and our glory and innocent ignominy, with so many ragged flecks of food stuck between our teeth as we smile and broadcast our imperfections to the world. This is almost unbearably poignant and moving to me, even as it threatens to trap a choking sob inside my throat for the ones who can't do anything about it one way or the other, and for the ones who for whatever reason won't even try.

So I continue to go into the Turkish mouths around me, according to the dictates of this constant imperative, making mental notches in an outlandish juggernaut chronicle and collecting evidence for a judgment I dare not utter. But somewhere behind this relentless oral fixation I feel the entire cultural weight and inertia of American advertising with its whole formidable armada pressing against me even as I'm helpless to stop it, an inertia composed of a colossal and dizzying superficiality that goes by the spanking brand name of a nihilism intent on taking over the entire world. I don't know how or when I became a prisoner of this ivory castle with its bars made of pure gypsum, but it's claimed me sure enough.

On the other side of these bars are normal, everyday people who don't have the means to do much about their teeth or so many other things besides, just like my uncle: the beautiful teenage girl on the city bus, for example, with long dark hair down to her waist and mesmerizing violet eyes who suddenly laughs out loud into her cell phone to betray the rusty piano keys rotting inside her mouth that hearkens some conflicting and almost shrill cautionary note, the old man sitting next to me fingering his Muslim beads with dirt-stained fingers, whispering to Allah as I catch a wayward glimpse of his cratered molars that look more like festering wounds, so many faces and mouths that keep coming and coming as I try my best not to stare but do so anyway on the sly, asking them in my silent and suddenly recovered, tiny voice for their forgiveness for my prejudice, which I'm powerless to stop and which makes me complicit in a thousand lies and crimes that have not yet occurred and are happening right now.

These Faces

The faces inside the back room of the old Catholic church just south of Boston are like cratered candles molded by grief: the flames sputter, nod, go out, come back again, manage to flicker on somehow in the long journey of bereavement that for many of them has only just started. You're afraid the slightest hush of air might blow them out. These faces all seem to say with one telltale expression that there's no hiding from the loss, a loss large enough to swallow each one of them without a sound.

Some are veterans, old pros, their children dead for seven years or more; others are brand-new to the keening, saltwater waves of grief, their children dead less than a month. The deaths come in every form: suicide, car accident, overdose, drunk driving, disease and mishap, drive-by shootings or falling from buildings. But all of them hang their heads in the same recognizable way just a slight degree off center, looking down into a place where most people will never go. I'm here at the request of a friend who lost his wife and first son a few months ago, but it's clear to me I'm way out of my league, a wide-eyed interloper who has no business sitting in on their stories. And yet here I am. The group is called Compassionate Friends, for parents who have lost their sons and daughters. The chairs are set off against the walls around a large table, covered with literature of every kind on losing a child; the windows look like they haven't been washed for months, maybe even years. The room is dark, with its mahogany furniture, and just as sturdy, the glass bookcases looking back at us in the dull reflection of gossamer panes.

One by one they go around the room and introduce themselves, telling the rest of us when their child died and how, in brief, matter-of-fact explanations shorn of any commentary and at the same uncanny volume, the words coming out of their mouths with a slow, deliberate sadness they've been treading since their child's death, like cosmic weather reports from the center of tragedy. They're mostly working-class folks, with Boston accents shaving off the *r*'s, one with eagle tattoos on his forearms and another with an oversized pocket protector, their hands useless and folded in front of them, as if they will never be able to touch anyone again without trembling or misgiving. The mother whose son died in a car accident can't keep from crying, but they are unlike any tears I have ever seen: they seem to well up from deep inside her like some eternal spring that's been waiting to flow all of these years. She can't get through her introduction, so her vacant and arrow-faced husband speaks for both of them in a monotone voice as if he's reporting from the moon: "Our boy Richie was killed three weeks ago by a drunk driver. He was twenty-two." And as they introduce themselves one by one, it's like they hand each other an invisible baton as old as the world.

I want to tell them how beautiful they are, how inexplicably round I find them and their countenances, the way some of their loping shoelaces communicate their grief in a way words never could. I want to touch the electric chord of their sadness one jolting truth at a time, not to fool myself into believing that I know what they are going through but because there's nothing else, no other action or gesture in the whole universe, that anyone can do. I want to let them know somehow what

witnessing their grief means to me, how this same roundness
I sense in the room is like so many invisible hoops coming
together just above their heads to partake of the only one and
infinite pity, the one that goes on forever into the heart of love's
mystery; I want to remember these faces and honor them somehow for what they are showing me and showing each other, the
ground zero of being human. They are unlike any faces I have
ever seen, that same roundness chipping away at the edges of
their lives like so many sharp scalpels doing their small work
in the drip-drip sadness that's become their daily routine of
remembering and living in memory, bolts, shocks, and patterns
of laughter and color humming inside their blood.

For there is no angularity in this room, no spikes or shards
sticking upward from the nimbus around their heads, nor do
I think there could ever be under these circumstances. Their
faces and what they communicate are inexplicably round
somehow, rounder than any circle. The sagging pockets under
their eyes are round, and so are the knuckles of their hands;
the lenses of their glasses are round, and the way they look
at each other and then look down at the floor during some
point in telling and retelling their stories. Even the Italian
woman who lost her son named Tommie is round, she who is
angrier and more bitter than the rest, angry at God and angry
at her family who has told her to "get over it" nine months
after his death, her diatribes and cuss words giving way to
ever more roundness that's already filing off the edges of her
woe even as she speaks. They fall like iron shavings into the
abyss in the ongoing and agonizing project of making her
perfectly round.

Now it seems to me that other people, including myself,
are blasé in their comings and goings, and have about them
something that's sticking up or sticking out that will eventually

succumb to this same roundness, the edges more or less resembling brittle clefts or cliffs that will finally need to go, judgments and assumptions sticking out like two-by-fours, with spiky waves of energy I have come to think of as illusory senses of being and innocence, perhaps even smugness. But not these grieving parents. Not one of them has a sharp angle left, because each one of their edges was blown to hell in the wake of their child's death. There's a geometrical aspect to grieving that I'm just starting to become aware of, and I'm learning it from these parents who don't even seem aware of my presence. Though I can't see this roundness or capture it in a photograph, it's the one ongoing constant that I sense in this room, the vital link between each parent and the rest of us who have not yet undergone the transformation of ultimate loss.

I look at my friend Joel and see that more than anything he's still confused, bewildered in the newness of his loss, his shattered pelvis just starting to heal. He'll walk with crutches or a walker for months, and doctors say he'll walk with a limp the rest of his life. His life is unspeakably different now. And he opens up to these strangers like a strange version of his old voluble self, the words coming out of his mouth without strings of meaning attached to them yet. The other parents look at him with complete patience and understanding, their faces ever rounder in the listening. What he's saying is nothing new to them, just keener in the telling because he's the newcomer on the block, the one who has the rest of his life to move through the stark murkiness of an overwhelming sadness. He's only thirty-three years old. His wife and first son were killed almost instantly when the cab they rented ran headfirst into a sand truck in the desert of Jordan where they had gone as Fulbright scholars. He tries to tell them this, tries to tell them other things, asks them if he will remember their voices or if that too will fade away. A woman with red hair and a haggard face assures him that their voices won't be lost, that they will sound again of their own accord when he is ready to hear them.

He tries to relate how it was, how he woke half a day after the accident to the news of his wife and son's deaths. He's talking more than anyone else, taking over the room with his painful monologues, but no one cares because he's really just talking to himself and they all understand this, putting the broken pieces back together again so they will crumble once more in his hands, as they will continue to crumble from here on out. The only coherence in his narrative is the roundness of his pain, the roundness of their faces, the roundness of their own memories that can only slope in the direction of love. Listening to their stories, listening to their questions and the laughter that temporarily alleviates the heaviness of their burden, I feel like the most privileged guest in the world, for what they have to say and how they have to say it circumvents all trivia and nonsense, each syllable and word carved out of their hearts. They can only speak of the dead with love, and they can only speak to each other with that same love, rounder than the constellations and all the revolving stars, the eddies and whirlpools out in the oceans and orbiting satellites that cause us to look up in wonder at the sky.

You could go into the past and future, into any time at all, and you would never encounter anything else that more fully means what it is to be human, what it is to embody and share the deepest kind of grief. I feel like they have taught me, are teaching me even now, the limitless boundaries of grief and how it is endured, how the roundness keeps coming back and blooming in the aftermath of their waking dreams. Some have lost God, and some have lost other relations because they can't share this grief: but none of them, I think, is lost to that rounding love that makes every other love possible. Perfect strangers, they love each other instantly and without hesitation regardless of race, profession, age, personality, or bitterness; they love without hardness, without the hope of recompense, without even a sense of self at all. It's big-time love, the real thing, the one that goes round and round and round without ever once stopping to count the cost or letting go of that same love that's slowly killing them each and every day.

Porch Falling

I watched the house burn down along with the others, but
what I remember is the reflection of flames dancing off the old
man's glasses. The windows of his eyes flickered with his own
catastrophe, pale reckonings that left them hidden, obscured
by the fire that ravaged the home he built, the porch where
he sat for hours, falling all around him in drifting ash and
shingle, roiling with smoke like a hell's mouth. I never did see
his eyes; they stayed hidden behind the glasses, which had the
odd but unforgettable effect of playing the destruction in twin
mirrors that rippled and leaped in counterpoint to each other,
the rhythm of the flames like two people running side by side
and reaching out to catch a passing train. It was his glasses
that made him real, and glasses that separated him from
the rest of us, shades that took him to an alien kind of place
where few of us had ever been. I had never before seen anyone
lose everything.

I used to walk by him each day, and every time he nodded
to me with a slight and genteel tilt of the head. We never
exchanged a word. They were oddly balletic moments, as brief
as a skittering leaf, punctuated by the wind chimes hanging
from his porch. More than a few times I was a little unnerved
by his constant vigil, as if he knew what I was thinking as I
walked by and could discern the passage of a beetle on a piece
of bark from a block away. Now I think he was preparing for

the fire that would take away the work of his hands, the stark aftermath of disaster. Now I think that to understand the power of fire you have to find a way to live inside it somehow, even in destruction, and that's what he was doing as he stood in front of his own burning porch, perfectly still, in perfect attendance to the fire. He was stranded on the island of his own awe, and no one could reach him. I thought of Odysseus, and of the blind prophet of Sophocles; I thought of other men and women I had heard of who lost everything, revered legends that become the deep equipment of our species. Here was blindness and revelation, blindness *in* revelation, those twin mirrors reflecting everything a person would ever need to know.

You'd think it was the fire people had come to see, the fire that was threatening to break out of its swirling hoops to burn down the house next door, but really it was the old man himself we had come to see, to watch how he took the invisible body blows of catastrophe in front of us, to see what he would do next, if he would curl up and shrivel away like one of his own family pictures in the flames. Who was he before the fire, and who was he after? What visions of the past did he have that were suddenly back again, bigger than any August sunset? I knew him just by watching him, knew everything there is to know about a person, not him as an individual, but as a representative of our species *in extremis*, everything apparent there on his craggy face; I saw the lines and fissures, the tiny clefts and moats, and saw moreover that he was completely still in front of the flames, not flinching or turning away.

If I waited to see him make a gesture that would betray what he felt and was thinking, I was wrong; if I waited for some timeworn trope that makes grief recognizable and even palatable, I was guilty of apostasy from the only faith that matters, the one that says we must continue to believe, even in the

destruction of who and what we love. I was just a voyeur twice
removed, watching a man watch the fire, waiting to see if he
would show some sign of what it might mean for him and
for the rest of us. But nothing developed in the tableau of his
stillness, as if he were carved out of flint like an arrowhead and
forged before the fire; he had been banished to a place no one
chooses to visit but which came to him in a sudden airborne
and invisible desert that had been hanging above him all along;
descending, it found the person of its arid choosing and wiped
him out from the inside.

Did I expect him to smile or cry? Did I want him to lash
out? Did I want him to shake his fist and curse the sky? I could
feel people watching him, the actual pressure of their eyeballs,
glancing at him furtively from time to time, and then it became
one, all-out stare like a kind of wall: such was the power of his
magnetic loss. You couldn't, wouldn't, take yours eyes off him.
I've wondered about this since, why he was such a riveting
sight, why his simple and profound stare, which we could not
penetrate behind those glasses, seemed to galvanize a neighborhood into waiting, a sacred kind of waiting. People who
lose everything look different than the rest of us, and once you
see them you know the one true and human universal face,
the noblest face there is. Suddenly, he became a guide to the
deepest part of us, for we knew — or so I interject backward into
the scene unfolding even now — that what we were seeing had
some kind of foreboding for each of us, telling us how our lives
were defined by what we cherished most, and showing us the
prospect of it being swept away.

For it had nothing to do with the house and nothing to do
with the fire; instead it was the simple way he held his own
body in stiff, dignified repose. I could take the memory of that
posture into funeral homes and car accidents on the side of the

highway; I could summon its bare-tree carriage into moments
when who and what I am is defined by how I stand before loss,
his unconscious legacy to me. We were watching the fire, yes,
but we were also studying the man we all hoped and did not
hope, prayed, we would not become: the person in the middle
of losing something very important, a house, a life, an ideal.
Like a rural community, like schoolchildren, we were waiting to
see how he would take it, and then to ask ourselves the impossible, impertinent, and necessary question, How would I react
if I were in his shoes?

I wanted to take his living example into my own losses,
whenever and however they occurred, though I did not think
of it then. I think of it now when the memory of the burning
house comes back to me in a blinding glare, the archetype at
the heart of the meaning of fire. From thirty feet away I could
make out the pockmarks of his scraggy face, scattered pepper
shots like craters on the moon, how no one then or ever could
fill those dark pits, how they emphasized the starkness of his
face and the sweat and oils of his stoicism. I took him for the
man he was, the man for all of us, the man we would someday dread to be. There was nothing else to take away from the
fire, no hidden consolation. I saw it on other people's faces,
which moved between the destruction of the fire and the old
man's face, his expression fixed in a stare-down with fate.
His porch was falling, the one he cared for on his hands and
knees, falling into the pathways of memory and peace, becoming something he would never have again without misgiving,
the smoldering boot heel of a god, leaving one overwhelming
question in its wake: *If we cannot lose what we love, then can we
truly love it?*

His porch was well beyond the reach of human touch; it fell
back to the first time someone lost something to fire. He stood

there as they tried to put it out, everything in motion around him. After awhile, maybe twenty minutes, maybe an hour, I took one last glance at the old man in front of his burning house, let the sight of him register inside me once and forever, and walked down the street into the summer night.

Shadows Moving Porch-Wise

In my old neighborhood an old man used to walk by every day humped over like an injured bird. I saw him sometimes walk up from the bus stop on Dodge Street in Omaha, the bald chrome of his head leading the way, or sometimes the absurd bill of a garish red baseball hat that parted the air before him, a thin gangplank of tentative feeling.

One day in winter I saw him bundled up. Snow swirled around his body in transparent lace until he seemed a descendant of some other world so much older than this one. He was the archetypal figure of all humankind in that uphill movement, treading slowly, so carefully and deliberately did he step out over the ice, a hooded man walking in winter always a return to earlier, more elemental forms. He was so darkly vivid then, his parka cupping the whole of his head, his bent figure alien in the white landscape.

At such crucial moments — when we see into the nobility and horror of a struggling figure, it is enough to know we're not permanent fixtures here. Enough to know the daily struggle in the body's own deterioration and waste and the need to walk it off when it's cold and snowing, when the body, pray, is not all that we would set store by. Something else is playing its quiet violin in the corner, down and out of the weathered husks of our bodies. I have had these intimations before, when my guard is down, or when I am deemed ready to receive such messages from an unseen force. Something strums the fine loom of our mortal strings, and we are temporarily cast out. I don't want my body to break down, now or ever; I don't want what is real, but it keeps finding me, seeking me out, ready or not.

Once in grade school a boy named Sean played kickball though his legs were horribly thin and mangled, like two gnarled sticks knobby with buds that would never bloom. When he ran, it was like a rickety sawhorse teetering back and forth, his head at the mercy of that fervor, lolling from side to side. We let him play and reach first base, even though it took him a while. He kicked the ball, then lurched forward in his braces.

Time slowed down then, became liquid in the aftermath of his grotesque, unfolding limbs; he crabbed his way down the faded line, rocking back and forth in braces he would use all his life. Nowhere before or since have I seen another person more determined to get where he was going, to try to outrun the poor wrack of his body. His was the bravest run. And he did it day after day, while the rest of us lost interest. I can still see the wind whip up behind him, a scatter of dry grass, the occasional puff of chalk that lifted like smoke. I sensed something was breathing down his neck — more, that he was after something himself. I could see it in his eyes, the need to get past you into the illusory, open fields where he could shed his braces and run.

Sometimes snot streamed across his face in a clear, delicate lasso, but he couldn't afford to stop to wipe it from his face, not with his arms extended to balance himself. I knew then, or rather now, after twenty-two years, that this temporary embarrassment about his appearance could not alter the trajectory of his spirit, which was constantly on the go. Why was he there, and why was he playing a game he had no chance of winning? His disfigurement was not a novelty, he was just trying to get on base. But seeing him run on that hard patch of scrabbled earth cut through all my Catholic schooling, bringing home to me the power of a god who could make bones like these even as he knit my own. I was not the elect either then or now, merely lucky. It was random chance on a parochial scale, an uneasy sigh of relief that others bear the burden of damaged bodies. This alone should have cured me of my smugness forever, but I seem to have to learn it again and again. His legs were the bamboo cage through which even now I can glimpse the terror of the universe; no walker, no cane, no braces can hide this naked view. I ask only to be spared this haunting glimpse from time to time.

Who knew his fervent, crippled running would be his lasting gift to me, his own will stretched taut in the face of the ineffable? People suffer: we learn this, again and again. But what of his choirboy's face and ashtray-thick glasses? What of his cowlicks raised by static and the manic click-clack of his knees? This was no Tiny Tim, no frail spirit; he hated you if you felt sorry for him, often showed disdain anyway just to spite the whole damn thing. He was after something else. "Sean's turn," someone would yell, and he'd step right up and take a whack at the ball, each time a breathtaking lesson in equilibrium. He and the humped old man who walked by every day are spiritual cousins, if not brothers. The rest of us, who walk just fine, look on as voyeurs who can never know what it's like to have our bodies twisted, to try to unbend a crooked limb. It's important to remember this. Sean was simply a gutsy participant, like the old man. Their bodies seem to be calling out in impatience for a chance to be heard, to move for bounty's sake.

While I'm parked at a stoplight downtown, a man walks across the street not five feet from my car; his head and torso are normal but his legs are stunted so that they look like they've been shrunk in a fire. They bow out in delicate arcs, splinters from a bone harp. Before the light turns green, he has to hurry up to reach the other side, his head moving back and forth while his thin, warped legs continue their delicate shuffle. He could not outrun the shadow of a tree. This is a case where laughter could careen into crying, where the varied and mysterious plight of human beings could move you to stock-still wonder and dread. *There, but for the grace of God, go I.* I try not to stare but stare anyway. I catch a last, sidelong glance as he moseys down the sidewalk, his torso meant for another body, his legs unfit for anything but walking under water; they seem to shudder with each step, a careful lattice of eggshells defying their own outer softness and delicacy.

Then he's gone, and I take from him only the tremor of a need that borders on the other-worldly. Who are we trying to fool after all, that we are safe and fine and that this is how things should be? What does it mean to be crippled or healthy, to notice the gaits of other people, their limps and listings, their football injuries and car crashes or the memory of childhood canes? My older brother used a cane when he was a boy, and I remember him then as preternaturally old and wise and shriveled, a frail kid smarter than anyone in his class. He paid for these differences dearly. As I remember it, he was mocked ruthlessly, and almost every week someone picked a fight with him because he was different, and every time — even long after he no longer needed his braces — he fought back and took a beating.

What does his boyhood crippling mean now, now that he has a family of his own? But the other man, the man whose legs and chest do not add up to anything harmonious, is doing his Motown soft-shoe down the walk, the arc of his body a sloping layer of shuffles. It houses his spirit in a way that can make you breathless. But moving, trying to progress, he could be any man or woman on earth blessed and cursed with locomotion, the body sometimes slave to the will, sometimes master. A common enough sight, but one capable of rocking your whole belief system, cutting through the debris of any false hope. We have always lived in a world where unseen forces play out every day, forcing this person to manage warped bones, that person to limp along.

We're like shadows moving across the bleached planks of a porch, any porch I have ever stepped foot on, with its slow sweep forward, the gradient progression. There is no turning back. Sean is a shadow moving across a porch, and so is the Motown man and his funky groove of doom, and so is the old man with his red bird bill and sunflower parka that hide his whole face from the cold; they are all shadows, warped at the edges, and I follow them into the curving darkness where bones bend to the force of gravity and genes. I have no choice in the matter. I don't see the old man much anymore; he is dragging his purse of recognitions behind him somewhere else. But I need him walking up the hill just the same. I need the shifting carapace of his humped back. I need Sean and the Motown man and my brother tottering on his cane. They come to me when I least expect them, when I do not see them coming, when I look up and suddenly here they are: crippled figures who won't stay still, each one of us like a shadow moving across a porch to the end of the boards where the motes burst into blinding light.

Falling into the Arms of a Dervish

Coming home from Turkey after living on the Black Sea for almost half a year, I feel like something's missing, but I don't know what it is. I keep looking and waiting for it to return in a flash of recognition in the oddest, most random and forlorn of places, on the bathroom floor under a rug for instance, in the wailing refrain of a garbage truck taking a corner at twenty miles per hour, in heat waves rising off the asphalt or a smoker's wracking body hacks, but so far it's nowhere to be found. So I keep waiting and looking, glancing with shy and furtive eyes into fellow American faces as if I'm seeing them for the very first time, at the snaky blue vein-work of an old lady's forearm at the grocery store, or the raucous laughter of tough-minded teenagers wearing their baseball caps hip-hop sideways, shoulder-dipping down the sidewalk. I keep waiting to see it or for it to find me, to grab me and clutch me with eager, loving fingers by the elbow and whisk me away to impart its loving secret, but it hasn't happened yet. And right when I think I almost know what it is so that I can reach out and touch it, it vanishes and moves beyond me, leaving only the smoke of an ineffable longing behind.

And to not quite know the thing you are missing, and to miss it at the same time with a joyful, keening, even madcap love and sorrow, is a strange kind of double, even triple whammy, something I never could have anticipated upon

returning home. I suspect I may not find it again no matter
where I look or go, even if I return to that mysterious and
beloved country that has already cast a lifelong spell on me like
so many sesame seeds sprinkled at the bottom of a simit sell-
er's basket. I know that such powerful and primary experiences
can't be duplicated, nor would I have the heart or audacity
to even try. All I can really say for sure is that the best and
brightest part of me is still back in Asia and probably always
will be, clumsy and fumbling around at the mercy of another
culture and every passerby, knowing just a few spare phrases of
Turkish and trying to understand and be understood, which I
now have come to believe is oddly overrated. Something of precious and inestimable value happened while I was there, and
not just to me: it was like the sudden flowering of an awakening that can't be relegated to just one person, which no doubt
partly accounts for the fairly hysterical tone and trajectory of
this headlong essay.

What I mean to say and almost breathe out in a cooing sigh
is that going to Turkey was like being spring-loaded and shot
out of my life to be emptied and filled and turned inside out at
the age of forty, going back to something I once perhaps knew
as a child in the light of a doorway or in the shaking leaves of a
tree lit up like a glowing roadmap to heaven that still somehow
got away from me over the years, something precious and outside time that kept popping up its head peek-a-boo style once
in a while that I never could quite get a bead on. I mean that I
came back to the states tenderized and fairly cooked, with faint
wisps of smoke rising from the top of my head sizzler-style,
that I cried and wept more tears of joy there than I ever have
before at the simplest gestures and overtures I saw or encoun-
tered, an old man moving beads through his fingers next to
me on the bus, a young woman who took my backpack in her

lap when I gave up my seat on the crowded *dolmus*, or shared taxis. I kept finding myself suddenly flooded with waves of gratitude and wonder and something very akin to a heretofore unrealized and unarticulated hope — with gradually but surely the strangely insistent imperative that this somehow needs to be told, somehow communicated — not because it happened to me, but because it happened at all.

Because it seems what we mostly hear about nowadays is the heartbreak, mayhem, and destruction that's going on all around us, not to mention the division and suspicion between peoples and nations that keep breaking out into war and genocide — rarely do we hear how the world is mending itself one human encounter at a time, how it can and is learning even now how to love and respect all its diverse elements from people to polar bears, that some motorists still stop on the side of the road to pick up turtles as they try to crawl across a treacherous highway, as I saw one woman do the other day in her stylish high heels. For whatever reason we just don't often hear about these things, and when we do, they're quickly drowned out by the seemingly more important and pressing issues of the day, which usually involves the din of imminent disaster or the latest tick- tock of doom's comeuppance. Many of these same issues — from global warming to acts of terror- ism — certainly do occur and need urgently to be addressed, but their very deluge seems to wipe out the reality of any other kind of exchange.

But these just aren't the whole story nor were they ever nor will they ever be, even if we as a species end up blowing each other into smithereens. And sometimes I think people don't really want to hear about love, especially between people of very different cultural backgrounds; they don't want to see it in each other and see it in themselves for a whole host of painful, legitimate or bogus, reasons. They don't want to see it because then all the walls and flags would come toppling down — they themselves would come toppling down. Because I know for a fact, for example, that there are several bus drivers in Turkey that I will meet again in the afterlife for the kindness they showed me time and again, for the brief, radiant views they offered me behind their drivers' seats with the whole city of Samsun in front of the windshield like some kind of sweeping, seaside panorama inside the flashing interstices of overpasses, a kindness that happened to me so many times that I started to suspect a subtle, even cosmic and beneficent, sleight of hand, a little divine tomfoolery masquerading as public transportation. Many of these drivers wouldn't allow me to pay the fare for reasons still unknown to me, perhaps because I looked so obviously foreign. So they let me ride for free, like any wide-eyed guest under the auspices of a host's sudden hospitality.

I know they were doing the work of angels and were gritty angels themselves, that no suicide bomber or greenhouse gas can mitigate the quiet, gentle light coming out of their faces or the way they took a corner cranking the manhole-sized wheel in their hands. I know they weren't rich and that they worked long hours, that they didn't have to be kind to me or make me feel like such an honored if somewhat bewildered guest. And though it will no doubt come across as a bit over the top, one of the most important things that ever happened to me was riding on a packed and crowded bus seated on the steps of the stairwell because there was no other room as the driver and I tried to communicate between stops, then coming up to a red light and a boulevard awash in sunlight where a city worker was watering a concrete median of tulips atop a firetruck's turret with a water cannon inside the enveloping mist and aureole of a dazzling rainbow, as beautiful as any dew-drenched dawn.

I thought then, even as I think now, it was more, much more,
than being a foreigner in a strange and distant land — more
than being the first American the vast majority of these Turks
had ever seen or talked to, or being the only westerner anyone
knew of in a city of over seven hundred thousand: rather it
was like the peculiar timing and circumstances of this place
and people served to open the doorway to the person I never
knew I was or ever had the chance to be back home, which
is one of the most astounding realizations of my life. I could
have gone my whole life without going to Turkey, lived out
the rest of my appointed days as a born and bred midwestern
American, faintly troubled sometimes perhaps but basically
happy and fulfilled nonetheless with a very comfortable and
privileged life, and I never would have known or experienced
the most basic but also mystical kind of human connection
that exists between people of any culture or ethnicity, walking
down the street day after day arm in arm with my appointed
tutor or *hoca* named Kadir, a young master's student who tried
to teach me Turkish though I proved to be a woeful student, or
running into the arms of friends in a parking lot just to greet
them or say hello or goodbye in the course of another day as a
guest lecturer at Ondokuz Mayis University teaching American
literature: I was always running into someone's arms the whole
time I was in Samsun, like the late college basketball coach
Jim Valvano looking for someone to hug after North Carolina
State pulled off a most improbable upset over a highly favored
University of Houston team in 1983. I don't mean to suggest
that this trip was not without its serious bouts of loneliness or
struggles or comedy of errors and rife frustrations (any westerner who has spent time in the Middle East will probably have
their own experiences of this, i.e., whatever you think is going
to happen, happens in a way you could never quite anticipate),

only that these kept giving way time and again to a vast but personal embrace that at times reached out to encompass the entire world.

And this sense of imminent embrace followed me everywhere I went in Turkey so that I never felt truly isolated or alone for long but usually just grateful and full of a sense of possibility, ready to reach out no matter who or what was before me, which was always changing and swirling before me. Everywhere I went someone was waiting to take me into their arms, from shopkeepers, friends, and colleagues to people in the streets — everywhere around me I sensed an almost delirious love closing in, the kind of love that has nothing to do with nationality or gender, nothing to do with distinctions at all: like some grand and immense tipping point of which I was just another small part of a huge and sprawling human chain.

I don't even expect this to be entirely believed because there are some moments, cynical ones it is true, that I wonder about it myself, and wonder furthermore if I wasn't just lucky to catch a particular human wave at a particular time whose very timing made it a one-and-done deal, never to be repeated again. But then I remember, no, that's not true: these things really happened, really touched me: I still feel the after-imprint of so many bosoms pulling away. Part of me wants to sing and shout about this above anything else I have ever known, part of me wants to announce in clarion call that whatever people are doing to each other or about to do or afraid of what the other will do, it's not so bad, even though it may in fact be terrible — that love still somehow manages to flourish in the most unlikely of places between the most unlikely of peoples and always has and always will. And here is my humble, if somewhat crazed dispatch as an imperfect testimony.

I was in an all-Muslim country and there was nothing to

fear. It happened this way. And no one doesn't want to be loved and appreciated wherever he or she goes — no one wants to go it alone in the desert that we are sometimes called to wander in, the desert that may be our very own lives, sometimes for years and decades at a time, sometimes as long as we're alive. I just had no way of knowing before going to Turkey that this same desert happened to consist mostly of my own beloved midwestern America and all that it entails, a region and country I can't help loving even if I tried not to — and that this same desert was all I had ever really known with a few brief stints to other places. But after just a few weeks in Turkey I came to realize that I'd been swimming uphill for most my life in Nebraska and Michigan, especially as a writer, swimming against an invisible current so pervasive and overwhelming that I had no way of knowing it was there until I was briefly airlifted out of it, looking back westward from a vantage point seven thousand miles away. There's nothing original about any of this, no one to blame, no good guys or bad guys: just the sometimes shocking and bracing clarity that certain kinds of far-flung travel can sometimes illuminate, leaving behind their own wake of epiphanies like so many spendthrift jacks thrown from a moving van, as I became increasingly marinated and then grilled — I don't know how else to put it — by the warmth and affection I experienced in Turkey.

It was like I kept falling into the arms of a dervish in the form of this or that person, and it never let up while I was there, that for whatever reason and impetus I was being embraced and embracing back for all I was worth, realizing more and more that, just like Rumi instructs us in one of his poems, "Live in the nowhere that you come from, even though you have an address" — my truest and deepest home is no place or single culture at all but each and every person

I meet along this mortal journey. And I also came to realize that being at the mercy of others, especially those from a very different background, is a very important and necessary thing to do — perhaps the last and final hope of this world in the twenty-first century. I put myself again and again in their hands — I had no choice — and I must report that this same vulnerability opened floodgates of love, wonder, and awe.

To my shame and consternation I haven't been able to realize this in America and I'm not sure why: I don't know what it suggests about me or where I come from, or how these mysterious and poignant things come about. But maybe it comes down to something as simple and radical as the willingness to walk arm in arm down a street with a person of the same sex and not fear that such touching will somehow be misconstrued. I do know it wasn't a fluke, just the truest, deepest thing there is for someone on this earth, the sense that he or she is both deeply connected to everyone he meets and also an individual, that such embraces can happen anytime, anywhere, and are in fact just waiting for us to welcome them. The truth is I'm a stranger in any country I visit, even my own, but it no longer matters that much where this strangeness takes me or wherever it may it may lead me, as long as I claim no greater allegiance than an open and vulnerable human heart. Such contradictions are exactly where people live the deepest, richest, and also most agonizing parts of their lives; it's in these same contradictions that one's soul is somehow forged and honed and meted out in the extensions of its own unattainable longing. I've always had this longing to a painful, even excruciating degree, which hardly makes me special or unique.

But for some reason this longing found some resonance and even partial fulfillment in Turkey unlike any other place I've ever been, and in such simple and even hilarious ways that it was like an embarrassment of the ordinary. I still don't know why so many Turks break into a run or what catalyzes such sudden movement, why before one class the students broke into a round of sudden applause and stopped almost as fast, how Kadir could tell me with great earnestness that he was starting a diet only to take me two hours later to a baklava place without batting an eye. The mysteries of code and conduct, ritual and manner, exert their own beguiling influence that I'm coming to learn can't be predicted, turning every earnest visitor into a wondering child once more. And maybe being a strict minority of one was the key; maybe by being so obviously other and at the mercy of others is one of the ways to truly realize this for oneself. Because each one of us becomes a witness, finally, only to our own becomings, which can occur in our own backyards or very far away. Because I couldn't disguise my blue eyes and sandy hair, couldn't fake my accent, I was marked and branded for exactly what I was, an American abroad with no Seven-Eleven to walk into.

You can go years ever so slightly out of touch with something of ineffable value — you can watch TV and cry at movies and laugh with your friends in a bar, and still not come close to understanding who you really are. I know, because this has happened to me. I was living my life as a well-off American, teaching at a small college, working on books and essays, which remain a great privilege and bounty in and of themselves. But as a person I never could have anticipated what Turkey would do to me, like someone or something took my soul and turned it inside out, and not just for kicks either: I started to see in all the people I met there a kind of shimmer, a kind of peace and afterglow, some kind of ineffable brightness that poured out of their mouths as we walked down a busy street. I kept getting swept up on some updraft current of human affection, with

someone always seeming to be singing a Turkish folk song in
the background, almost all the way to the vortex of a hope and
brightness I've never experienced anywhere else. And now only
the odd but pressing and almost keening question comes again:
Now what? What am I to do with the fact of all those embraces?
I don't have any answer, just the burning dictate of a charge
that commands me to say yes, it really happened this way: Yes,
I am, you are, everyone is love incarnate whether we choose to
recognize it or not. Yes, we are home-stung and wandering, yes,
it's always time to fall into another's arms right now this very
second, whoever they are and wherever we may be.

3

Hope

Town

For several years now I've wondered, with a slow-burning ache, if I'll ever be able to chronicle and somehow give voice to what it's like to live in a small town in the middle of Michigan that's struggling to hang on, if I can somehow take the trains passing through night after night, offering up their long, drawn-out wails, or the water tower standing above abandoned oil fields and the rickety porches on the south side of town, and make some kind of sense of them, if only to myself, in order to say this is what it's like here, without heat, without sanctimony or censure or the least trace of sentimentality.

Because it's very important and perhaps even critical to say something about a town like Alma, to arrive at some under-standing of it even if it's partial and imperfect, to tug on the sleeve of the cosmos and inquire as best I can after this particular tiny corner of its staggering debris field and set forth an accurate but loving portrait about the place where I have lived for almost eight years now. How I came to be here from Omaha, Nebraska, to teach at its small liberal arts college isn't that important, only the fact that enough time has passed for the spirit of this place to slowly fill me up so that I'm starting to drip invisible drops of runoff that appear to the naked eye like someone afflicted with bouts of unaccountable sighing, sudden bursts of exhalation that suggest resignation or ennui but which are just a way to maintain a healthy level of stability in the midst of the town's continuous outpouring of lunar moon vibes.

To start with I must mention the storefront windows downtown I'm quietly convinced are unlike any windows in the world, though it's tough to justify why. You don't really look through them so much as they frame your entire existence in some as yet unnamed and ghostly dimension no one has ever defined. These windows ache when you appear, and there's no way to escape the gravity of their reflections or what they have in store for you, how they do the work of x-rays that connect the living and the dead in a continuum that goes on forever. I realize such radical claims border on the preposterous, that they teeter at the edge of good taste and would test anyone's credulity, but after years of careful observation I must steadfastly maintain that this is what happens if you look long enough into them. If I had the power I'd invite you to stand a few minutes in front of Macy's Men's Store or the Cobbler Shop to see for yourself this same glass, plunging down into fathomless depths with your continued stare and seeing how these windows manage to lay bare the soul of the one gazing into them, how around these reflections is the aura of a gray sky pressing down, and how passing cars' brake lights offer only a fleeting glimpse of reprieve.

I also need to mention the tendency of litter and blowing trash to flock and gather in startling and even catastrophic numbers in the fallow fields behind Wal-Mart like torn paper birds with the ink of McDonald's and Taco Bell printed on them, punctuated here and there by itinerant trash bags that manage to play their ragged arpeggios if you're close enough to hear them. This is a distinctly forlorn and landlocked type of music usually reserved for wandering mystics, the kind of music that draws its inspiration from the spectral wastes of a

manmade void. But above the fields and its legions of piping
trash you can still watch the pastel bands of the sun going
down over a distant tree line, as radiant as anywhere in the
world, and know that God and beauty are as mysteriously and
abundantly here as they are in the fading twilight of a Tuscan
vineyard or in a wineglass filled with Chardonnay glowing on a
sunlit table.

The Big Boy's at the northern edge of town isn't for the faint
of heart either, its fifteen-foot monstrous man-doll out front
holding up a burger the rough circumference of a tractor tire,
his garish expression so demonic and naïve you can see it for
miles around, lit up by a search light driving its wedging V deep
into the night. To sit in a booth at Big Boy's in the middle of
winter is to come in contact with something so overwhelmingly
sad and American as to be indistinguishable from facing your
own mortality in the form of a chocolate milk shake or a trip to
the salad bar arranged on a melting bank of ice. A child's seat at
Big Boy's is a plastic chip off a meteorite, the ketchup-stained
menus so many bendable placards from a place in the rough
proximity of exile or missing children.

A few years ago I sat in a booth at this Big Boy's and watched
the traffic going by on Highway 46, the headlights of the cars
and trucks on that two-lane highway so hypnotic it took me
several minutes to remember where I was. The red uphol-
stery of the booth was like a giant man-eating conch shell, or
monstrous ribbons of congealed blood somehow turned into
cushions. I looked slowly around the Big Boy's at my fellow
diners and was moved to realize that we all had come here for
whatever reason to eat and stare out these same windows, a
little lost and dreamy above our croutons and banana sundaes.
Did any of us have the slightest idea what being in this Big
Boy's meant? Was heartbreak ever more subtle or more teeming

with an unbridgeable longing? These aren't quaint or harm-less questions but among the most important ever uttered, not because it is I who ask them, but because they're waiting for each one of us to somehow come to terms with them wherever we happen to be.

The radiant, startling truth is that a small town like Alma burns eternity into your soul and it won't let up, not for love, not for time, not for walking the dog at midnight. It burns slowly in the faces I see around me even as it makes smoking tinder of my own waking thoughts and visions. I can hear it as I eat a cheeseburger at the Main Café, crying at a frequency beyond any known decibel. I watch the blinking salt trucks in winter spray their minerals over a blanket of snow and feel the fine, gray fanning out of an odd reassurance; I smell the effluvium from the giant feedlot eight miles west of town haul-ing aloft its invisible clouds of apocalypse in early August and I touch the weathered hands of the farmer's wife counting out change at the farmer's market under an awning buffeted by a gust of wind, where all the homegrown fruits and vegetables I could ever want to eat are displayed, and I know that this town has done a number on me in ways no map or primer has ever charted. I'm slowly pulling into middle age here, which I don't rightly know is a good thing or a bad thing, only that it is. I find myself unaccountably and inexorably drawn to billboards advertising 1-800 numbers for pregnant teenage girls and hot-lines for bad credit and giant pictures of mud-covered ATVs, tooling around on my bike on hot summer days through the trailer parks out of sheer wanton curiosity and even esteem, loving the lonely dirt roads just outside town for the dust they inevitably raise and the calls of cicadas and birds sounding from their hidden grooves and folds out in the fields.

I like going to the Shell gas station to buy wine and gasoline, to pay for a Beaujolais where deer jerky is for sale on the counter and old pickle jars with handwritten signs ask for donations for children sick from leukemia, to look out the wide, plate-glass windows in late July and see fields of sunflowers raising their delicate throats to the sun only to droop back down once the day is done — or to drive by the legion of deer that come out to feed at twilight next to one of the busiest streets leading into town, traffic and these graceful ungulates living peacefully side by side within feet of each other as if some agreement had been struck between them and underwritten in paradise. Such strange incongruities have cast a lasting spell on me, one I feel I've only lately started to get some clear-eyed purchase on. This town is burning me up and I'm starting to show signs of sizzle stripes like a human piece of charbroiled steak. I could live here for the rest of my life or leave tomorrow, staying or going not all that important somehow despite the incessant tug-of-war between the two that has slowly stretched me out in a gradual crucifixion. My family hasn't come to visit me and I'm secretly glad of this, for I don't think I could handle the subtle but relentless psychic pressure of trying to explain the inexplicable and tell them how I've come to live here or what it might mean, which is no one's fault, not even the town's.

For whatever reason and whatever cause, I'm not the kind of person who chooses where to go, but one who only submits to the place where he is bidden. I've wondered at this many times, how I end up in the places I do, occurring less out of volition than some other appeasing fate that bends me to its will, places like Miami, Oklahoma, and Samsun, Turkey, Wroclaw, Poland, and Lincoln, Nebraska. I've been called to live in this town for however long and let its river of dreams run through me in order to offer a report of what it's like, even if no one cares to read about it.

Somehow I've always known this, and guarded it like a secret that isn't mine to understand. I'm not supposed to fall in love with the beautiful dark-haired girl behind the dry-cleaning counter, but I need to be in quiet awe of her and carry this awe forward like the lit end of a Lucky Strike. I'm supposed to notice and say how I can already see the middle-aged woman she will become, the beginning of incipient lines around her eyes like the faintest crinkles of wrapping paper that aren't even lines yet, just the gentlest forecast of a sorrow years away from happening. I'm grateful for her beauty and the flashing tiny doors of her perfect teeth, the wrinkling sound of my newly pressed clothes in the see-through plastic, the fact that she knows what I smell like and the fact that this will never be mentioned between us.

Intimacy is such a hushed and heartbreaking thing that I think it happens between strangers every bit as much as it does between lifelong lovers, sometimes even more so. One day, for instance, I was running in the woods down by the polluted Pine River when I saw two men in camouflage outfits, one of whom was kneeling down in front of the other engaged in the telltale bobbing of fellatio as I ran as fast and loudly as I could on past to the sudden startled yelp of the standing man who had his hands on the shoulders of his ten-minute lover, knowing that I had accidentally interrupted an act that was strictly between them and their own relentless fantasies — and eternity was burning each one of us up even then, sparing no corner or aspect of our souls as the beautiful but sick river flowed on past down by banks littered with debris.

I never saw the men again, nor ever wanted to, but I can still hear the standing one yelp and gasp, can see the flashing whites of his eyes and the astonishment that signaled his instant understanding of the reckoning that had suddenly

found him on the trail and was just as suddenly gone, the
stranger that knew of his secret though he had no way of
knowing that I didn't or couldn't judge him for it. How fast
can desire or lust turn into something else, into terror and
remorse? Running past I saw in a revelation as big as my life
the standing man pulling up his pants like he was hauling
in empty fishing nets, gathering into his hands a sorrowful
impotence that lapped the town and his secret life of coming
to these woods so he could drop his pants, for coming to these
woods so he could come, for getting in his car or truck dressed
in hunting gear in order to achieve the release and climax no
other corner of his life offered.

I didn't feel scandalized, didn't feel anger or outrage, just
sorrowful and continuing wonder that these things happen
in a town like Alma and happen everywhere, that the men's
camouflage outfits disguised nothing, only revealed a deeper
truth. In fact I was almost grateful to see them, almost glad that
I could run on by within feet of their undeniable postures, that
the trail I was on gave me room to get around them and room
to keep on going into trees filled with shaking wires of lemon
light toward the teeming, hoarse-throated chorus of frogs that
sounds every March back near the cemetery in a low-lying bog.

This town has given me so much and also taken away almost
as much, some of it good, some of it troubling, some of it
defying the confines of category — fish heads nailed to garage
walls and cars and trucks parked on front lawns, tornado
sirens sounding the first weekend of every month in spring
and summer, and the hoods of SUVs strapped down with dead
deer. I've seen monster trucks driving by with Confederate flags
frosted into the rear windows, I've seen the geese come and go,
honking their messages to the sky — have seen how the seasons
change the town into something holy and almost everlasting

and the quiet reverence of the first snow blessing the houses and the lawns and the city park where teenagers go to try out new tricks on their skateboards. I've stood over the sluice gates of the river and watched the sun go down in a mist of rainbows, have walked home drunk more nights than I can count from one of its two bars smelling inexplicably of dog hair and smoke — have pledged my fidelities to the town and revoked all citizenship, pondering its formidable black-eyed ugliness and just as astonishing beauty with those same passing trains calling almost every night for all these years.

Someday I'll say goodbye to this town or it will say goodbye to me: we will come to a mutual understanding that need not be discussed, only inferred. I'll offer it my slowly cooked flesh and it will add it to the greater universal fire, or I'll take these same third-degree burns elsewhere in the configuration of an inscrutable enigma. I'll walk down some other sidewalk in another town or city, waiting for my life to catch up with me even as it does the slow, steady work of termites beetling through the webby darkness of my flesh, knowing that any place is good enough to die in and good enough to leave, that any place has the power to shake and remake a person into something he could never know before. I'll keep walking then and I won't turn around because I know that wherever I go, the way is always forward toward a place that is no place at all but a state of being filled with gratitude and mercy in the inescapable headlong leaning of home.

Army of Wonder

Lately I've started to notice a small army gathering momentum in a strange, gentle, and almost surreal way, an army that most would like to ignore, made up of people whose hands must be held while walking across the street, who can't buckle their own belts or wipe their own noses, who laugh and drool without provocation and do not carry weapons, and whose collective cowlicks would light up a midwestern city on the static electricity of their uncombed hair. They don't have marches, and they won't defend the slightest mound of earth — in fact, none will ever rise beyond the rank of private or even know what rank means; rather they live and move in a world of their own visions and utterances, a world few of us have seen and one that has always troubled me and drawn my attention, as if they are human doorways into the sun.

This army has no power, and some are even helpless before the complexities of a spoon. Maybe they're not even aware of how other people see them, but I have started to view them as the most important army in the world, the one I am supposed to notice and salute and perhaps one day join through accident or decay, the one that came together only by the mutation and splitting of genes and the grace of God. They infiltrate supermarkets, sidewalks, drugstores, crosswalks, churches, synagogues, cafeterias, hospitals, sporting events, schools: they go anywhere a civilian goes, and are usually accompanied by someone who watches over them. I have started to notice them because they're everywhere, and so many seem to share the same qualities, wide-open mouths and distorted limbs, sometimes with a shining white light emanating from their saliva. The light is pure wonder, glory shining from their eyes: nothing in this world will ever dampen it.

One day I saw what became for me their helpless and diminutive leader, a girl or woman no bigger than a bundle of firewood being lifted out of a special car seat by her father on a cold, snowy day. She was making sounds to herself in the parking lot, strange warblings and gurglings and sighs that sounded like hope to me, like incomprehensible words of praise. Her glasses were huge, transparent lollipops that magnified the world while making her small and delicate head seem even smaller. Something about her face was horribly wrong, her jawbones emaciated and her skin paler than milk; but what I saw beyond these almost made my knees buckle, for she truly was one of the most beautiful people I have ever seen for the light I saw coming out of her eyes. They shone so brightly above the painted lines of the parking lot and the laces of swirling snow; they shone out over the rest of the shoppers who were bundled up and hurrying to get inside or close the car door and speed away; they shone in a clear white light, blessing everything in sight, a beneficent, impersonal, radiant light that loved what they saw and touched. When I saw her, I stopped in my tracks: something of eternal significance was shining out of her face, eternity itself in the warped body of a deformed young woman who resembled Stephen Hawking. Her hair seemed one wisp away from blowing completely off her head, but the light in her eyes, the light.... I shivered, but not because of the cold. Desperately, I wanted that light to shine on me; I wanted her to look directly into my eyes and uproot every falsity and fear,

all the things I was so good at hiding, the core of my own cor-
ruption. Her damaged body was like a bundle of unlit candles
glowing from the inside, white candles set in the sun. Her burly
and mustached father was patient with her, pushing her into
the store in a wheelchair as he shopped. Like someone led by
an invisible leash, I followed them into the store.

For a second, for a brief moment, I thought I saw a ray of
light coming out of her face and from the clear windows of her
eyes. She was blessing a can of green beans in aisle five just by
looking at them, and blessing the hand of her father who took
the can off the shelf; she was scanning and blessing the labels
of the neatly stacked food, the hot sauces, the Cajun mix, the
rice and beans, and the dirty hem on the dress of a little girl
who raced past us. Her head lolled back and she blessed the
fluorescent light filling the store and the Muzak coming from
invisible speakers with its bland heartbreak, and the feather
duster stuck in the back pocket of the grocer punching prices
into a calculator. She blessed a crate of large double A eggs and
the grocery carts and the hard rubber wheels and the sough-
ing sound they made on the scuffed linoleum. She blessed the
bloody apron of the butcher behind the soundproof glass and
the scales weighing out hunks of beef; she blessed the dead
eyes of the frozen fish and the bags of pink shrimp — and all of
it registered in the calm white light of her eyes, blessing them,
blessing her; hers was a vast, constant blessing and benediction, and I wanted to be a part of it, to be lifted up out of my
own life and preoccupations into the wonder and light that she
bore witness to every day of her life.

What was it like to be like this, to have a body and limbs
so delicate they would crush like eggshells underfoot? Did
she know what she was giving to people like me when we saw
her, horror mixed with yearning? Could I learn to love like

her father — or learn to love what she knows and sees and the purity of that same light shining from her eyes? The truth was that she was already living in heaven while the rest of us were stuck down below, even if her body resided in hell and the crushing laws of gravity: I saw heaven in her eyes, if only in an almost imperceptible light, and I knew in one instant that everything I've been taught and absorbed about normalcy and bodily perfection is wrong. Here was heaven in the form of a warped young woman in Ashcraft's grocery store in the middle of Michigan on a winter day.

I don't understand the challenges she has to face if she is still alive, and the challenges the rest of her army must face, or the challenges they pose for those who must care for them; I don't know the ways in which they have been blessed and cursed, rising above or sinking below the rest of us. I only know what has crept up on me almost unawares after years of encountering them, my hidden and shameful secret, to see what they see and know what they know, the direct and unpolluted line to wonder, even if I had to become like them in body and mind. How could I join this army even for a day, how could I learn to march to the beat of this praise rising up from the wellsprings of their hearts? For I know they have been given the keys to heaven and they walk down its corridors unfettered and free, blessing everything they see and touch, even as the arrangement of their bodies and minds makes others recoil. I watch them and I already know: they have been struck dumb by the wonder they see and the wonder they inhabit.

This past Christmas Eve I saw it unfold in front of me. In the two pews ahead of me at Mass I saw an older couple and their severely retarded son; the man had a rigid military bearing and stood ramrod straight, his back like a pressed board. At first I did not notice them, but gradually I began to realize that someone close by was periodically crying out with delight, sounding like a human and hybrid bird, at turns laughing, sighing, cooing, and groaning: they sounded in part like the early songs of Hildegard von Bingen, seeming to express no words at all, but rising and falling on scales of a beautiful peace. Every ten seconds or so the human bird in front of me would make some kind of sound, which rose over the nave between the readings and choir singing. What began as a kind of embarrassment suddenly turned into an exquisite balm, a healing and a recognition: it seemed to me that only this retarded man was capable of expressing the kind of wonder appropriate at the first sight of the Christ child, the wonder that could not be expressed in words. I drank in this sound and waited with private eagerness for each new outburst; I had been thirsting for this sound without knowing it; I had been waiting for someone to come along and make the kind of sounds a so-called reasonable person would never make, hosanna cries and warblings. I projected wildly: I saw or rather heard this bird-man in my own house, in my own rooms, cooing and crying out periodically throughout the course of a day — and myself next to him or in the adjoining room. We would find delight together, he would share with me the discoveries of the ordinary, he would moan with joy over the sight of a bright red bird outside, I would rise into the wisdom of a second childhood, he would instruct me in the ways of praise and show me the doorway into heaven where I and the rest of us would swoon, shudder, and stare with ceaseless wonder into the light that made each one of us to conquer our bodies once and for all.

Guardian of the Lost Bell

The first awakening and the first hour out of sleep is the hour before dawn when nothing moves in the winter landscape except the wind lifting the bare branches; then, for just a moment, I think I can almost hear the after-ring of a bell tolling from far away, the one stroke that rings in the tone of pure honey, begotten out of a clear white light. If I could touch this bell, if I could somehow fit my life inside its tone, all would be made clear and I would be filled with understanding. I hear, or want to hear, this one bell tolling in the distance; I stand in the middle of the room, looking out the window onto the snow-covered world, listening for it.

The bell is not new, nor ever was: it could be a sleigh bell or wind chime or a two- ton bell in a chapel; it could be a bell affixed atop a baker's door, the bell hanging off the fringes of a baby's hood, or one dangling from a cat's neck. Or it could be the dinner bell my mother used to ring to bring us in when my brothers and sisters and I were children. I remember the bell: it was bronze colored, the size of her hand, with a handle made of polished wood. I think of her and it as one. I remember seeing her from far away ringing it in summer twilight, her other hand shading her eyes from the sun and the sound of the bell lagging behind her hand's motion, as if there was the briefest separation between her moving arm and the ringing. Then I became pure running boy racing for home, paying attention

to nothing else and closing the distance between her hand and
the sound coming out of it.

Never before or since have I been so responsive to a sound,
as if I was being called not only to dinner but also to something
else more urgent and important, the alarum sound of self I
would someday have to face. There was hunger in our response,
but there was also abandon in the way we left our projects; no
matter what the level of our engagement in play or clay experi-
ment, when we heard the bell it was all over. We bolted for
home as if our lives depended on it — and maybe they did, as
maybe they do now. My mother taught us this — and I wonder
if she even knows that she was training us for something else,
to drop what we were doing when the bell rings for the only
thing that could give our lives meaning. Sometimes she used
the same bell to call me in to administer my weekly allergy
shot, a ritual that bound us together. She'd ring the bell and I'd
come in hot and sweaty; she'd wash my arm and swab it with a
cotton ball dipped in rubbing alcohol, then pierce my skin. She
never hesitated, never fumbled with the needle. I watched her
face the whole time — and in her calmness I too was calm and
took my shot without a sound. "There," she would simply say:
"All done." And if I hear in those words even now something
of vast import, as if these shots were a rehearsal for something
monumental and even terrible, who could argue with me?

I want to find this lost bell and take care of it, the one who
makes sure it is burnished and bright. I look for it in the
mouths of tired women in the checkout line at the supermarket
with their kids in tow; I look for it when I'm stopped at a red
light late at night during a snowstorm and feel the hushed intimacy of blowing snow. I look for it as I run across the frozen
river when my footsteps are the first to leave a trace on this
path of water where no one has ever run; I look for the bell in

ashtrays outside public buildings, in the lid of a cardboard box flying out of the dumpster, in a baby's hand reaching out from a carriage, in the chocolate Lab chasing her own tail, in boiling water, in Gregorian chant, in the clear windows of a woman's fingernails. I look and listen for it everywhere every day but I can't find it.

Where is the lost bell, the one I heard in childhood at summer twilight, the one I heard yesterday walking across fields of snow? Where did it go? Can anyone tell me? Does anyone know? We ring the bell at different points in our lives without even knowing it — we ring it when our hearts are true and wounded, at the most intimate and hopeful times of our lives. Even though the bell is lost, it's been known to show up in unlikely places, in the shape of an envelope or the echo of laughter. If only we knew where it was so we could reach out and touch it, hold it up to our ears. But I know that's only wishful thinking.

One night it happens: I wake at three a.m. and get out of bed for a drink of water. I look out the bay window in the kitchen onto the winter landscape in the light of a full moon and the snow is waiting for the sound and appearance of this lost bell, the least bud and hubcap, the fenders of parked cars; everything is filled to the brim with this pregnant sound. The tolling of the lost bell is about to begin. I look around the kitchen and see hints of it everywhere: in rinsed wineglasses, enamel teacups, in a half-emptied jar of honey. Why have I been looking for it in only one place, only one form? The first time I heard the bell I was already ancient, and the last time I heard it I was four years old again — and the next time I hear it I will stop believing that it was ever lost or ever gained but instead right here in the stunned present. The bell is sounding for the one who yearns to hear it, the one who's willing to drop whatever

he or she is doing and run toward the source of its ringing.
It's ringing in the schoolyard and it's ringing in the homes of
people on Pine Avenue; it's ringing in the Masonic home and in
the crazy old man on his three-wheeled bike hauling his grocer-
ies, in the rafters of the dark gym and in the cemetery down
by the river, its peals no less urgent for all of this, calling each
one of us to move toward this sound as if nothing else matters
so that when we finally reach it, we will know once and for all
what home is in the silence of our hearts.

Bus Stop Elegy

Sometimes I want to get on my knees and pray, to what or to whom, I do not know. This need comes over me when I notice something, when it registers, when observing and listening assume their proper depth of attention and everything else falls away; it doesn't happen very often. It has happened three times on buses. I have stopped asking why this can be a charged ritual for me. I suspect causal links, but I cannot chart the coordinates. I only know that suddenly I find myself sitting alone on a city bus with folded hands, waiting for the invisible wheel to start turning and reveal itself as faces turn their countenances to the sun.

I get on, pay my fare, and hunker down in my seat to fade into anonymity, falling in lockstep with a kind of urban choreography. The other passengers interest me even if I try not to stare, and there are moments when I feel more intimate with this transient, shifting group than with anyone else I know. Some days, the bus seems to glow from the inside out like a tram made of windows moving through a stream of flashing billboards. It rocks gently and no one says a word, and I look at the faces and don't want them to notice me watching them because they seem almost noble in their tiredness and woebegone stares, which, of course, they are; and for just a moment, a touch lighter than a sparrow's feather falling in the attic, I sense something transcendent in this urban rocking and movement, and the whole weft of it is incandescent, lit up from within, a complete awareness of what this movement is, down to the hangdog imprimatur of gum pressed into the floor. It doesn't happen very often, and to try to tell someone of what you sensed just a moment ago seems not only ludicrous but outside language entirely, except perhaps in the delicate bone dance of a wind chime. Gone, it's gone, the moment it hit you, and you knew what it meant, it's always gone, leaving you groping for answers.

We rub our arms, let our hands dangle like dumbbells, shuffle our feet, stare open-mouthed, waiting for something, anything, to fall into our laps; we stare out the windows, which are the first and last refuge of the commuter. To believe another world is imminent in the most everyday of circumstances, to believe it exists at every bus stop in America, is to be on the road toward home, to the only place that matters. Home and city buses, home where I've never been, home is the promise of this ten-minute commute; I press the colored seal for my stop, the bell sounds, I stand up, wait for the bus to come to a complete stop, and get off. And whatever I thought home was, in the deepest reveries of nonsense, vanishes as I walk down the street.

If only I could get that Indian out of my head, the one rummaging through a trash can near a bus stop on Park Avenue in Omaha, Nebraska. His face was cratered like the moon, a topography so bloated and bleak it would make the staunchest moon walker shudder. His acne made his face one large, blimpy sore, a porcupine deprived of its quills. What tender fingers would touch that face, what hands would navigate the sensitive nipples and grease? I pictured a beautiful nurse coming to him at the end of his life with cool dry fingers, brushing them gingerly across his cheeks, his forehead, the bridge of his

nose, healing them before death so that he could sigh his last
with a kind of benediction. I'm reluctant to bring him up: he
approaches a modern caricature, a wasted Indian, slumping
near a bus stop, wearing an overcoat like a moth-eaten tarp,
with ratty canvas tennis shoes, so down and out and blotto he
is nearly a part of the trash he is picking through. He slowly
sifts through a wire mesh garbage basket, one affixed to a pole.
Paper debris got sucked away in the wind as he worked through
it. He is so careful and studious, as if he is inspecting butterflies for a collection. A bit of scratch and sniff, even a taste here
and there, he is fastidious in his threadbare collecting, he is a
molten lump of cooling magma hardening into stone. I watch
him with morbid fascination, marveling at his sleek black hair.

Home is where the heart is, in permanent transition, the heart
slowly stoking the fire of history: but here it has burned nearly
down to nothing, a wobbling candle flame threatened by a
blast of cold air. Just another park bench near a bus stop, just
another bleak moment in a midwestern city. I see buses as
moving pictures now, directed by fate where the cast is real,
revealing a city, any city, in its rocking and socking panoramas,
quotidian, sad, and always mysterious. Is it typical to watch a
drunken Indian sift through a wire mesh trash can in search of
a meal or a tidbit? I caught a glimpse of him from a bus window
as we stopped at a red light, and I don't know anything about
him but what I saw, a nation's history magnified to a pinpoint
of black hair and tatters. I watched him, saw him for the first
and last time, thankful to be on the other side of the glass. I
can't believe this happens every day; it strains the best part of
one to see it for what it is, a void into which a tiny human voice
is crying. One day I get on the bus, like any passenger anywhere; the next I am backtracking fast to get away from what it

means, how buses and bus stops can be holy places, why they keep coming back to haunt me in waking visions.

I get off at my stop at Forty-eighth and Dodge in Omaha a bit disoriented. Now where am I? What was I supposed to do? What am I doing today? What about the harelip who knew the driver personally, lingered like an old friend at the turnstile, swiveled the toothpick in his mouth? Or the wrinkled old black woman with the southern accent who hummed a gospel tune under her breath and kept saying in a singsong way, "My, my, what a fine, fine day"? Strange to think I may never see them again, that they are cut loose and adrift in the same world as I am, and may tonight laugh or cry themselves to sleep or rock in the arms of a loved one, or alone. Strange, I never see folks like them out in the suburbs, holding hands and singing songs. And really it is like that, a silent spectator sport, the things that keep gnawing at us for years that never reveal themselves all at once, but one precious glimpse at a time, one by one, on a bus for goodness' sake. Strange to finally recognize it for what it is, to ask ourselves what it means if it means anything, to wonder at the people who stand at the margins holding on to their hats and basketballs. No one fully knows what a bus stop or bus ride will contain, no one can predict its patterns, because the passengers won't stay still, as they turn with dangling shoelaces and bags from Target. I drive or walk by them at the speed of ignorance, watching people get on and get off buses, each step a little closer to some mysterious truth.

Every Day a Flower Opens

Another tiny old woman in another big city, this time Chicago; another sunny autumn afternoon where I wander the streets half-hypnotized with pedestrian movement and the pulse of its hidden necessities, down alleys and sidewalks in which I see myself in tinted windows and shingles of hung glass, around bins of open garbage and the occasional lost soul talking to him- or herself, through the hooped earrings of self-mutilated youths who are more worldly than I and alien in their worldliness.

I realize now that she shows up every time after a bout of feckless wandering where I find myself caught up in a pace that was never mine to follow. This time she is Korean, with close-cropped hair and an oversized backpack, who might fit into a teacup, with a gimp in her left leg that signals either a balky knee or cartilage worn slowly out of whack until she assumes a sea roll or the rocking gait of a sailor. I look up from a gauzy meditation and suddenly there she is, shining in the sun. She's about four and a half feet tall. I follow her at a tentative distance, measuring my steps. And what do I hope to learn this time, what can I take and use from this diminutive guide? I can't get too close or our bodies might burst into confetti.

The grains of such moments are tied to an ineffable longing; they disintegrate anyway upon inspection, but they must be canvassed, gotten into somehow, as if they were hollow seeds radiating a pure white energy; if I could, I would crack them open with a thumbnail. The woman and everything she represents is already disappearing as I try to get it down, and yet I would celebrate her and my hesitant pursuit because they change each time, inexplicably and forever, my own forays into the meaning of hope, of redemption, of how grace works. Like Rilke's violin, I encounter a version of her everywhere I go, playing a tune composed out of the wet ink of old age and urban legend; but how quiet the sound is, so soft you could almost mistake it for sadness. The timpani is like a string of water beads bouncing silently on the membrane of a savant's inner ear. We keep taking steps over the sidewalks and the curbs, over the scent of roasted peanuts, around a man who dangles a minaret dancing to a cranked-up Victrola. None of it makes much sense. We walk past chain stores entire blocks long that will never love anyone, past parking meters and dark cars nosing out of alleyways, beside traffic that contains the echoes of waves but not its tumbling shadows, past blowing scraps of paper advertising 1-800 numbers, hair loss treatments, diet pills, psychotherapy.

I follow her. I follow her past Diversey Street going north, I follow her past the neon and blinking signs of liquor stores, wholesalers, drugstores; I follow her into the hollow spaces of my own heart where I am a kid again walking dread-ridden and hopeful that sometime soon something of this mysterious winding way will make sense, will weave together into a tapestry I can hold in my hands; the world in her wake is suddenly so beautiful and so ugly that the contradiction threatens to rip us apart, each day, every hour. I watch her take tiny steps on the sunny side of the street, and a vagrant trash bag suddenly rises up like the hood of a headless moon goon; she walks under and through the floating debris, the candy wrappers from last night and the soggy catalogs smiling at no one from the gutters.

I follow her. We walk through the cigar smoke of a potbellied merchant speaking Russian into a cell phone, we walk around twin Chihuahuas on a chained leash whose eyes were taken from the woods of eternity; we walk together in single file, she leading the way, and she makes me think of all the old women I have ever known in my life, the women whom I have never been able to thank adequately, the women who crush me with a sense of inadequacy for everything they have done for me, the meals, the stories, the best kind of comfort that people know how to give, kolaches, syrups, anecdotes in foreign accents. I follow her. I am her grandson at a far remove, light years away, and I am trying to get back to a place I was kicked out of so long ago that I can catch only a whiff of it sometimes: a stray reminiscence, something like a pinprick. But I will never catch up with where she is going, though I'm willing to chase after her to the iron gates of a cemetery. She is already receding to a place I cannot enter, a collapsing human star, a death trap, somewhere beyond the borders of any known country. I can't go there. I can't get in. And this sense of suffocation, of time running out when something was beginning to make sense, hurtles me into a chant I can't stop saying, that nothing is lost, that kindness and gentleness last forever, that now more than ever is the time to praise, even if I don't have the words, that I must keep repeating this to myself for the rest of my life to keep their examples alive. I need to keep saying this to myself always, like a punch-drunk acolyte who mouths the words of a catechism he will never understand.

Every day a flower opens; every day someone folds the clean laundry or hangs it on the line. Every day someone is singing in the shower and making the first pot of coffee; every day the sun is changing the geography of the clouds and trying to break through somewhere. These are incontrovertible facts;

we chew on them in sleep while others drift off to death. This ancient Korean woman, whose face in profile is grooved with smile lines, is not really looking ahead; her hands are folded behind her back under the pack so that she looks like a little philosopher contemplating the roots of an obscure Korean character whose translation might be something like *shoe* or *tree*. She is working it out amid the labyrinthine streets where I follow behind, sheepish at this secret need to see what she is up to, not the secret of why are we here but why does this tiny glass bell keep ringing in the middle of my chest to remind me of something I can't put into words? If only I were given one sign or chance, an opening somehow, I would catch up with her, bow down in front of her and ask, What am I supposed to do with this ringing, Mother, this silent bell that keeps tolling? She doesn't need this, of course; how absurd to think it could matter one way or the other, that it matters, period, except in some slight and hidden way. We're strangers after all; we're from different times, different races. We will never meet again — have, in fact, never met to begin with. She is a blessing to these teeming Chicago streets, and that's all I need to know. She is already rising on a catafalque of flickering light; she is already coming out of the aching shell of her body. But the moment this perception hits me, it vanishes, and she disappears around a corner.

I let her go. I let her walk away. How many times must this happen, a near encounter that was no encounter at all, which nonetheless changed the ions of my thinking? I stand near a mailbox as people hustle past. I am hollowed out like a drum. And what strange sound begins to vibrate there, what strange hum sent through the invisible teeth of a mouthless mantra? Every day a flower opens, every day a seed drops into an invisible crease. Someone is remembering a glorious night before, someone is falling in love. Every day the blinds are parted by someone hoping to see the sun, looking for the vehicle that will take them to a special destination. Every day a leaf blows over a parked car like a tiny map of some glowing geography, a radiant, translucent hand. Every day the first sip gives someone courage, a little pleasure, some hope. Every day a sick person discovers some new reason to live. The Korean woman and her invisible sisters, gone into the dust, gave me something crucial without knowing it, continue to give me when I least expect it, when I am out wandering and alone with the world at large, never realizing that succor is waiting around every corner, in a tiny figure of strength and fortitude beyond the boundaries of prose where I wait every day to rediscover the light, papery weight of grace.

Washed Away

I have seen them coming as if in a dream, the single mothers with
their kids in tow, the old ladies and migrant workers, odd bach-
elors wearing dirty imitation sheepskin coats — how they come
in carrying loads of soiled garments, wanting to make them clean
again, wanting to make them fresh. The ritual is quietly amaz-
ing, like a threadbare grace. Can anything match this for simple
clarity, the hope it produces in small baskets of cleanliness? The
Mexican man two washers down knows this. He's dropping do-
rags into the washer one by one, paisley bandannas like leaves
from a polyglot tree. He's dropping them into a contemplative
stew of physical labor, broken English, telenovellas. I see it in
the careful way he moves, the dirt impacted like icing into the
seams of his torn jeans. He's lowering his personal rainbow on
this cold Michigan night. He's slow and fastidious in his task, on
the opposite shores from shame. The grooves in his face are like
flint, his hands stubby and work-honed, the chips of his fingernails shards of hard candy. I'm under his spell and wonder where
it will lead, the dirty clothes, my handkerchiefs, the head-worn
pillowcase; I wonder how the clean laundry of home really works,
how its crispness finally signals, at long last, my arrival to where
I was meant to be, in carefree rest or dying in my sleep, among
people who will not judge me, in the slow seepage of sunlight
moving from room to room as I lay with my eyes closed, hearing
the laughter of children playing in a neighbor's backyard.

Kids run down the aisles to play video games in the corner. The manager pushes a mop and stops to shake it out over a trash can. Dust motes float over the open container. People fold their clothes, separating lint and combing out the wadded tissues and toothpicks that have found their way into jean pockets and hooded sweatshirts, shaking them out and stacking them in small bundles that will not stay neat and folded for long, that will topple in the back seats of station wagons and vans and rusted-out Pintos rumbling like cage rides at the state fair.

We're surrounded by the swallowing darkness like a small craft of fluorescent lights careening through space. The hyperclarity of the moment confirms the eternal strangeness of everything around me, cereal boxes at the grocery store and their indices of ingredients, the inflatable Santa outside a tire store, a woman walking down the side of the road on a foggy night carrying one of her shoes, the wince of small stones on her face. It all comes together in the Laundromat, the mystery and vividness of half-apprehended things, disintegrating like mist in my mind.

The solace comes from doing ritual tasks in a bright room, in the smells of clean laundry, in the sudden bloom of hot air from an opened dryer. It makes me wonder what else I have missed in the way of public blessing, in strangers doing simple things together, in sharing and not sharing what we have to do in order to live an orderly life. Changing the oil. Walking into a bank. Buying a candy bar. Where do our lives meet and come together, tightening the net we cannot see?

I sit in this public place in a white plastic chair and look around slowly. I feel the static cling of other people, I sense their lives unfolding in ways I cannot fathom out of the range of understanding. If only I knew what it meant, then maybe the waste I perceive inside and outside myself could be part of the fabric that could not be divided, turning and folding and connecting everything where the spaces between threads are momentary loops before they touch, wrap round each other, merge, become one. But it's just a Laundromat; it's not a waiting room to the infinite. Dust bunnies crouch in the corner waiting for a puff of air to send them drifting in a soft caress. There's mystery in that, an unbearable beauty. But the infinite will have to wait, even if it does show up here in small glimpses, in the browless eyes of the dryers, staring back in maelstroms of swirling colors. Before any of us can be washed away we have to make a mess of things, screw up our lives, get wine stains on our pants; we have to carry almost everything we own in navy bags and plastic tubs and bring it all in to be thrown into the rough and tumble of permanent press, the rinse cycle, the blasting heat of the dryers. We're chained, like Simone Weil says, to necessity; and that necessity here and now is a seemingly endless cycle of dirt and hurt, tattered sleeves, shirts that have seen better days, urine-stained underwear. Coming to know this even gradually is like finding a secret but overwhelming hurt the size of a small egg, tough and shiny in the lining of one's own heart.

We wash clothes and fold them, we take them home, we take our loneliness public, we bare it in bright places for anyone to see, to compare our loneliness with the loneliness of others and to arrive at the only certain knowledge we can have, that we can't know what others are feeling and thinking, even when they try to tell us. We can't know. Here in the Laundromat, that's okay for now, between the various cycles of washing and drying: that's the way it is. Maybe someday when the time is right, we'll bring in just ourselves stripped to the waist or naked — the Mexican man, the obese mother of two whose belly stretches out to the width of a washer, the student who's tuned in to a distant radio playing in his head — and we'll know finally what we have been practicing for, every ritual leading to this, every defeat and worry, each moan of pleasure and disappointment, every dripping faucet: we will be ready to be washed clean until we glow like a little girl's sundress hanging on the line.

Working in the Jewish Cemetery

We put the bones in a small pile in the middle of a cobbled path so we wouldn't forget them, about half an acre away from the mass grave. A few stood over the pile and talked in low tones for awhile, uncertain of how to proceed, somewhere between recognition and disbelief, just a few degrees shy of open awe. The bones were moist and sand-laden, dark in the gritty way that buried things tend to be. No one knew for sure whether they were human or not: we surmised that some had come from small mammals, while others were too big and familiar, almost certainly human. They felt like heavy wooden flutes in your hands.

We agreed it was important to keep them in one place, in a more or less informal pile. No one knows where this idea came from, a long dormant and atavistic fear or the abiding sense that there was no other way to handle them with respect. Then the spiked vibe of discovery was over. We drifted back to work one by one, almost regretfully, feeling the magnetic tug of the bones' spent energy. Although I didn't say this to anyone at the time, seeing and holding them was a revelation to me, like brushing with my own fingertips the blueprint that makes us human. I wanted to touch those bones and I wanted to bury them, wanted to hold them up to the light stippling through the trees and invoke the Hebrew prayers of the Jewish dead whose language I don't understand. But that is good for nothing. What mattered was the simple but brutal work we were doing, clearing paths of vines and thickets dense as jungle underbrush, picking up trash and empty vodka bottles, burning the wood that had to be cut down with a chain saw.

I realize now that I was as good and useful as I will ever be working in the cemetery with a shovel in my hands and a bandanna wrapped around my head, not because I was a part of cleaning up this vandalized Jewish cemetery in Wroclaw, Poland, that had been neglected for half a century, or because I had any special cause to feel righteous about it, or because teaching and studying the Holocaust gave me any profound insights into genocide, but because the hard, backbreaking work of restoring this crumbling and teetering place slowly and painfully put me in touch with the dead in a way nothing else ever has, the digging and the beauty of the cemetery like a piece of broken glass to see through all the way to eternity in rare glimpses and flashes, a shutter opening for a second before it closed again to the sounds of traffic and the cries of invisible birds. Sometimes I would look up from digging and notice the canopies of trees wheeling high above, the leaves shimmering with such urgency and loveliness that I felt on the verge of some revelation, waiting for me to be still and pure enough to see it. Then I knew what peace and fulfillment were, if only for a moment — the humility that comes from honest labor in the service of a cause that has no truck with individual achievement. Sometimes I didn't even want to go back to the States, didn't want anything else but what the Jewish cemetery had to teach me through silence and graffiti and shovelfuls of earth, through the long neglect and decay that slowly turned it into the site of a growing awareness.

To say I fell in love with the cemetery wouldn't quite be accurate, because it would suggest that I had somehow come

to claim it as my own when just the opposite of this is true:
instead it had claimed me, had worked its way into my body
and memory like no other place ever has. And some days I did
find myself asking the fantastic, almost preposterous questions:
Why not spend the rest of my life working in this cemetery that
had already become a part of me like a secret ache, so precious
and dear that I can't think of it without gratitude or regret for
what's been left undone, the paths that have yet to be cleared
and the overgrown headstones, not to mention the mass graves
at the northernmost end? Why couldn't I make of shoveling
a life's work and vocation, giving up my house and job for the
difficult task of working in a place that others have dismissed
or forgotten? Almost always the questions came in the wake
of a simple clarity, something noticed and seen after standing
up from digging, the way the sunlight filtered through a single
poplar leaf, filling it up like a flattened cup, or a headstone
leaning off to the side and curved like a bell as if it were just
resting for a decade or two before it stood up straight again, the
cobbled, uneven paths and the way the light sprinkled down
here and there in pools of shimmering gold.

However you cut it, it wasn't a bad place to be or to work,
no doom or gloom at all but rife with a kind of mysterious and
playful humor that kept popping up at odd moments, peeking
around corners and announcing itself in subtle ways, the giant
hare playing hide- and-seek under some bushes before it disappeared, the birds that sang down from above, the marching
band you could hear starting up every day at noon, the collective *Oy vey* coming up out of the ground that nobody could
hear. Although it's tough to prove, I always had the second
sense that the dead found our work a little funny, perhaps even
a little too earnest, though they blessed it all the same in their
copes of growing dust, hearing every complaint and cussword

when something didn't go quite right or the gossip between
the students, the dead's all-encompassing listening bigger than
any full moon. I'm convinced the dead have a sense of humor,
and you bathed in it gradually each day as you walked among
them, waded in this calm but threatened sanctuary even as you
struggled to make sense of what it all could signify.

Is that what we mean when we say the dead are always with
us? Is this why I sometimes had the sense that they were playing a good-natured joke on us with cosmic overtones?

What a shock and a commonplace to realize the dead are
untouchable and yet must hear everything you do and do not
say, blessing you somehow whether you're aware of it or not
without passing judgment or popping up out of their graves to
scare the hell out of you. You could do worse than to spend the
rest of your life digging in a Jewish cemetery or any cemetery at
all, brushing off headstones, listening to the birds and discovering how the dead listen back at you — you could do much,
much worse, with everyday ambition and greed, worries that
bear no fruit as the oh-so-serious and dire world goes about its
dubious business of self-preservation, crashing stock markets,
international conflicts, presidents who come and go, billion-
aires flying around the ocean in hot air balloons. After a while
you get the sense the dead don't care much for these, not out of
any harsh disdain, but because they've discovered something
lasting and true and aren't about to give up its secrets. So I am
drawn to them, and keep going back to them not even knowing what I'm looking for but still sensing it nonetheless, almost
hearing it, loving it because I can't touch or hold it or describe
what it is.

But they do. They always have. No skinheads can take it away
from them by their hate crimes, not even the ones who, two
weeks before we got there, pushed over a wall in the cemetery

and spray-painted "Jews go back to Auschwitz" on the grave of
Clara Sach, who died in 1913. That's important to know, maybe
the most important thing ever, that even human hate and
idiocy have their limits, including my own, and that such will-
ful ignorance and blindness will be checked at the door before
I myself am lowered in the ground or burned up in a furnace.
I found something in the Jewish cemetery in Wroclaw that
I've never found in America, no matter how much I love the
U.S. and where I'm from: the roots of a place that has started
to grow in me and all the people I've never known who I've
become close to nonetheless, like a universal family that has
taken me into their homes to work for a time while they get on
with the everlasting business of being dead. It's not as morbid
or creepy as it sounds, more like coming back to the place
where a part of you has always been. It was important to be a
nobody in Wroclaw and not know the language, to walk the
streets anonymously, to be dirty and invisible on the streetcars
returning from work, to be tired and hungry, to have to wash
your clothes in a bathtub and hang them on the balcony — not,
I hope, out of some kind of misguided slumming but something else completely.

I still don't know why this was so important, only that it
was and still is. The reasons slip and slide past each other,
morphing into different explanations and scenarios, each
one as plausible as the next and therefore just as expend-
able — because it's good and simple work and no one would
could dispute this (who would argue against cleaning up a
cemetery?), because we were visitors and therefore already on
uncertain ground, there just for a month; because life was dis-
tilled to a few bare essentials that you could carry on your back;
because the room we lived in at the Jesuit Dom were simple and
threadbare with no distractions, fit for monks or inmates, the

church bells chiming every half hour as you heard people singing between readings broadcast over a loudspeaker. Because
of these and countless other subtleties that planted in me the
almost heretical notion that maybe, just maybe, a quiet life of
simple service is the best one can hope for on this earth, even if
it takes place halfway around the world in a country where you
will always be a foreigner or a gentile twice or thrice removed.

Could I really give up everything to work as a kind of grave-
digger in reverse, digging to make sure the graves were clearly
marked and taken care of, so that visitors could reach them?
Could I really give up my salary and teaching job, the house I
had recently bought, the new life I had started with the woman
I love that I had left for a second time to come all the way
over here? Could I really spend the rest of my days under the
tutelage of the cryptic Mr. Wyechko, the sole Jewish-Ukrainian
caretaker of this thirty-acre plot who doesn't speak a word of
English so that we communicated mostly through gestures
and smiles and sighs of frustration? What was it about this
place that had pierced me? At best these were almost selfless
thoughts — at worst, projections of a maudlin self-indulgence.
But what is true is that the cemetery did a number on me
and I don't think I'll ever recover, its crumbling and grafittied
walls like a humble invitation to be broken again and again by
its beauty and the tragedy underwriting its long neglect, the
knowledge bearing down that something of inestimable value
is waiting for you inside if only you will go there and be among
its ruins.

You go your whole life never knowing what it is, only that
it's there, waiting for you to catch it in a glance or will-o'-the-
wisp, to believe once and for all that some ineffable presence is
somehow there, waiting for you to acknowledge it. And that's it.
That's all. It's gone almost as suddenly as it comes and there's

nothing else, no other consolation or revelation, no profound
truth speaking from the grave or ribbons to pin on your lapel,
just the solid thrust of the shovel into the ground and yards
of appalling work ahead of you. I don't know even know what
I was supposed to learn after going back to Wroclaw again,
just the peaceful presence of the dead you never knew in this
life, Herr Steinman or Frau Goldman turned to dust long ago
and the strange resonance that hovers above you like a perfect
tone of waiting, that follows you after you've gone back to
your so-called normal life, an echo that is no echo at all but
which sounds throughout the rest of your days. And I hesitate
even to put it this way, because it sounds so overreaching and
grandiose, a quasi-titillation with death, when really it's just a
decaying, teetering cemetery in eastern Europe with no Jews
left to take care of it.

Is it strange to think such work can do this to you — do this
in you? One can only live out the questions and hope to answer
them someday, the Jewish cemetery already turning into something else with every passing month, changing in my mind as
I change along with it, Mr. Wyechko becoming like a ghostly
second father to me who comes back in my dreams. The bones
were just a part of it, small, scattered fragments orienting
themselves like metal shavings and pointing to some cosmic,
utter north that can't be refuted. They were only the logical
result of making progress toward the back wall where there was
evidence of human habitation in the form of makeshift huts
cobbled together with tarps and flattened tin, surrounded by
a debris field of slashed rubber, frayed wires, and broken glass.
Thugs still come in now and then to steal the headstones to use
in Catholic cemeteries, making off with them in the middle of
the night, requiring at least four men to load a single one into
the back of some Yugo.

There's nothing to keep them out, though the cemetery is
officially closed to the public every day but Sunday. There are
only a few hundred Jews left in a city of close to one million,
and most of them are old and dying. Mr. Wyechko is the only
one who watches over the whole place, and he isn't getting
any younger. Occasionally a retired policeman named Marek
will help him out, his bushy mustache reminding one of Lech
Walesa. But the cemetery is losing ground to the encroaching
city around it, becoming more and more an informal dumping
ground and place for transients to live before they drift on to
some other place. The reality of this is beyond the reach of pity
and grief — beyond anything I have the power to name, only
that the tides of Wroclaw are lapping at the cemetery walls,
eating away at them, breaking them down brick by brick, stone
by stone. So spending time and working there and then coming
back to the States creates this bewilderment, a tearing and
rending so delicate and soft that it can only be called inevitable.

All you know is that you are different somehow for being
there, and though you want to take this difference back to
America and let it live on in some other perhaps more dramatic
form, the truth is, it probably won't, not as fodder for activism
or speeches or a new way of life. Maybe it'll be just a piece of
melancholy you carry with you wherever you go, maybe just
silence or wistful gratitude for the place that touched you so
deeply before you left it. Christ said to his followers once, Let
the dead take care of the dead. But is it possible that the dead
can somehow take care of us — or at least touch us enough to
make us love each other whether we're Jewish or not, black or
white, Muslim or Christian? Is this what any cemetery has to
teach us, that the dead aren't bent on vengeance and haunting
so much as a simple peaceful waiting that unfolds forever?

I don't know. I don't think I'll ever know. But I'm no longer afraid of dying — or rather, no longer worried about what happens to my body after I'm gone. They taught me that at least, if only for now, before I forget it again, only to have to keep learning it over and over. They listen, they wait, as small animals and insects scurry over them with the sounds of the raucous city above but somehow also far away in its daily rhythms of traffic, drunkenness, shouts, and sirens. Then it's quiet again, it's almost safe — it's almost what you would imagine a neglected cemetery to be, poised for the myriad small events that slowly turn it into something else, the dead feeding the roots of the trees that look down on the rich and the poor, the sick and the broken-hearted, with equal acceptance in motes that form columns of veiled light shifting minute to minute before they're eclipsed and go out.

Latecomer to Glorious Places

Every place sings in someone. And every place hums a live bright wire in the air above its crown that's tough to touch or hear except for the one who was born to be jolted by its unique electricity, which cracks the soul like the skeleton hand of a lightning flash lighting up sheets of place. Like these small dunes off a state road in northern Michigan where I walk alone today, calm in the almost cocky knowledge that some creature is watching me from the woods.

I wish it well, whatever it is, badger, fox, or deer: one glance from any one of them is enough to know all of it is good. How could it be otherwise? Something watches all of us with a tenderness we can hardly fathom, and it is not of this earth: its eyes are made of everlasting and it never stops staring. A bear growled once nearby when my wife and I ventured too far into the thick brush of its territory. We hastily apologized and hot-footed it back the way we came in a rubbernecked power walk. The bear said *far enough* and we heartily agreed. But today I'm out in the open in the sand, and the wind is burnishing every-thing there is, even my own blood coursing in my veins. Let the flies play hopscotch on my head if they want, I won't begrudge their brief matchmaking in my hair. I didn't know it was pos-sible to be this full of joy walking and looking without knowing the names of the trees — I didn't know this love affair with the near north would blossom and continue to deepen, changing my perceptions and my life in the space of a few wide-eyed months, months without beginning or end but sheer constant shining through and through to the fevered lips of a goofy grin.

Let others have their mojo and renown and brand-name clothes, let others have their camera phones: I know this walk will be with me in eternity and that this breathing is bread, the ferns glowing in the woods I just came out of in slow-piped radiance over the hushed forest floor, so lush and abandoned still they must hide a thousand scurryings of praise. It's unlikely that this should happen to me, for it seems more a legend reserved for hermits and beggars and boys who grew up with the wolves. I don't know what to do with the inscape of this ecstasy but hold it as long as I can or put it in a patched-up sock to wait and see what else may happen. But one glistening pebble in the middle of the road is enough to make me say yes to the pell-mell fact of this wonder spilling out all over, a wonder I felt as a kid a few times but which went into hiding the older I got. Now I'm tempted to walk around barefoot and carry a handmade flute, now I'm convinced that walking in a place like this can bring you to your knees, that the fact of sun and wind and sky with trees rocking on their trunks is too beautiful to gussy up and too real to imagine, too sere in the mystery they embody and too *are* to ever take lightly again.

We don't really deserve them, not by a long shot, for many of us still regard them through the stone-cold lens of utility: we see them only as potential furniture or whatever else they may do for us, pieces on a chessboard. The history of the state rests largely after all on the back of upright chairs and four-poster beds. The proof of such colossal and continuing disregard is even apparent here in the red and yellow paint slashes that mark many of these trees for clear-cutting two years from now, as most of the woods I just walked through will be chopped

down to the height of my knees. When we will ever learn
our lesson, I wonder? When will we ever grow up to become
children of wonder again? I suppose generations have always
grown up in a wilderness of tree stumps, but it seems a poor
legacy to leave behind. But today, this one day, I won't dwell
too long on this doomsday knowledge; I won't allow the echoes
of encroaching chain saws to turn me away at the gate of the
kingdom I've been so late to come by, the kingdom that has
been here before I was and that will be here long after I and the
ambitious follies of our race are gone. There's peace in this, but
of a woebegone, even haunted kind: these trees have already
made me nostalgic, and I just left them ten minutes ago. But
perhaps it doesn't really matter anyway: no matter what we do
or do not do, when it's all said and done it's only about light
and love and a certain windborne levity that dapples the fronds
of the wild bushes and flowers, so many open and waiting
hands that perhaps the whole world is sustained by the readi-
ness of these flat-heeled palmings that also see and stare and
do not look away, that announce their presence by a gorgeous
kind of waiting agog at the fountainhead of so many gravity-
bent rays.

I teem and thrum on this walk, alive to the least pint-size
marvel, and this is the miracle of being here and not somewhere else, even in thought. If ever I were a nail driven into the
very heart of things, it is right here and right now. How can I
turn my back on this world ever again?

How can I drive away and put it on hold for months at a
time?

I try my level best not to think about it when it's time for us
to go because we are so fortunate to have such a place to return
to, and yet an hour after we drive away I know a part of me will
remain here at the edge of these brief and wind- torn dunes

with meadows and bottomland falling away to the south and trees rising up in the north, and the calmer, saner, and better part of me at that. It's not even a choice, but the magnetic pull that holds me fast, geigered to the spot. There's nothing new or original in this, nothing overtly dramatic: all I can do is turn my pockets inside out and keep walking and say thank you to the sky. It's true I've grown a little quieter inside since these environs have oozed into me, a little more conscious of reverence and something I can't quite name, aware of my tiny, infinitesimal part in the larger whole, a whole that somehow despite the odds keeps inviting me back to explore a few more feet without recourse to a map. No one could claim this place as remote or uncharted, no one could say the sand here hasn't been trod by a thousand feet before me. But somehow that's beside the point, an afterthought for some feckless accounting that cannot wrack up this dearness in any ledger. I feel like a forty-year-old bride with stubble on his chin and a sore Achilles tendon as I start to give myself over to this vast and mysterious spouse that makes rain out of its eyebrows and touches me with fingertips made of gossamer and spider webs spanning the dew-drenched leaves in places I have never been.

I do not wish to leave him, I do not wish to let her go when I have just arrived at this late and brimming hour, a latecomer to glorious places. But since we've come to live here part of the year in Roscommon County I have also come to feel the encroaching sense of a profound limitation growing in the choired chambers of my bones: I know I cannot bear such joy for long in this current human form, only bolt by bolt of gladness, which I cherish. This, I think, is what makes being human particularly hard sometimes, even disorienting. The glory can't be held for long before it turns into something else, something grasping, vain and selfish, even ultimately destructive. Like all love, I will have to let it go — and in letting go, suffer the knowledge that it is past and already fading, even as it is somehow assured forever. The contradictions deepen with every step, and every time I return I know a part of me has never left, the part moted for paradise singing psalms in the twilight hue of a passing cloud.

But before too long I'll be standing at the drugstore downstate buying bottles of wine as one of the panels of fluorescent lights blinks and sputters, threatening to go out, with dead insects littering its U-boat-like bottom, large grains from a bitter harvest. I'll watch this plank of soul-robbing light and think of the sand up here and how my feet sank deeper into it as spores of thrumming trees drifted across my brow, tiny parachutes of bright loveliness on a still lovelier errand that carries the fruit of the continent and the guttural laugh of lovers deep in subsidence after lovemaking, blossom upon singing blossom that blesses the earth and moves about like so many blown kisses with weeping strands of silken hair stroking the air back in a soul patch's tickle, the almost unbearable raspings of a coming communion.

The story goes that we live to strive and be successful, to take care of our families and each other and take on challenges, that we live in order to become someone, that God is waiting for us in a temple or a pew with light coming through stained-glass windows on the Sabbath or Sunday. I officially quit the very last of these as a cloying dogma here, now, forever: let someone else take up the mantel of this doom-laden frivolity if he or she wants, I am shut of it for good. A handful of sand here slipping through my fingers is enough to know that there is no church but unbounded sacredness everywhere, that crickets betoken angels who chirp out everlasting mercy if only we would hear them with our hearts and without judgment, that to rest awhile under an unfamiliar tree is to somehow participate in the awareness of the infinite and ongoing divine that beckons with the chlorophyll of every living plant.

Simone Weil wrote that our primary sin is our inability to feed on sunlight, and I have to agree with her. But even that tragic recognition is tempered with the tug that we can sometimes taste it from time to time, our throats threadbare chutes of yearning that, despite every rebuff this world has to offer, still refuses to give up this divinity. I knew this when I was four, and I knew it before I was born. The banquet's still laid out in a shaft of sunlight on a windowsill in a high-rise downtown in any city, or in a gleeful cry from a woman down the street in the lettuce-light of her voice, still here, now and everywhere, all the time at once, if only we would bow to it. There's no porthole so small that it can't get through, no drop of rain unaided by the sudden sluice gate of its deliverance.

I don't want to live in abeyance anymore of what I know is true and real, or pretend I don't know that I'll suddenly combust one day into a million blinding sparks that will go back to the oneness that they were promised to. Like Czeslaw Milosz in his poem "How It Should Be in Heaven," I've been to paradise and listened to its birds in its season, shortly after sunrise. And I know it will trail behind me everywhere I go from here on out. This is strange and new to me but also familiar somehow, as it must for each one of us if only we would have the courage to walk away, bestowing an almost eerie calm, for death no longer seems like the worst that can happen but only the price of the ticket to go back for good — to go where being is, where the light and the sand and the trees are one and I am no longer apart from them. One of the animals watching me knows this, one of them frames my whole existence in a startled stare that touches what it beholds for an instant, then disappears deeper

into the brush. The twenty-first century cannot love us, but
no century ever has nor ever will. Better to be a refugee and an
outcast, better to be misunderstood and a perpetual outsider,
than to betray this vegetable, animal, and living knowing that
deepens with every season. The sands have blown and gathered
me here for an afternoon, and this is enough because I am here.

I wish I could ask this lover a few questions, I wish I could
tell him and her how much this means to me in a language
washed clean of words. Who are we to do these things, I'd ask,
painting the trees: who are we to forget how all of this is connected, how we are connected, how a man or woman walking
alone is the paradigm of the betrothal lapping at our heels,
combing through our hair in brooms of gusting air? What are
we missing and why is this missing so rife with misunderstanding, the assumed superiority of our destructive race? Is it
too late, have we gone too far?

But I'm a hypocrite, like everyone else. I haven't gone nearly
far enough in what I know is true, and as Thomas Merton says,
if you do not act on what you know, then you do not even know
it. No, these questions will not and cannot do: they are back
there where the headaches and judgments are, the madnesses
and the ceaseless chatter of newfangled machines that widen
the gap a few feet every day. The wise among us live out on
every kind of margin, and what they finally have to say can only
be heard by those who are likewise outermost, even rejected.
They walk along like seers of the trembling air, and they hold
no flower that is not dear to them. They don't own guns and
they don't want to be famous, and they keep their hearts in tattered matchbooks where the flame is always imminent, always
ready to flare up and burn out when the least glory calls his or
her name. I knew this tribe in another life once, I think I was
briefly one of them, gypsy-sorrowful and rhapsodic to the core,

with a violin made of coat hangers and poems made of glass. I am late getting back to them — and the tabloids are full of headlines that never change. But I've been blessed to know a place that's different, where right and wrong have no purchase and the law books are buried for good, where the threat of noise is still threaded through with bolts of silence and trees beggar and pull at the roots of the sky. Nature will find a home anywhere, in a Grateful Dead T-shirt or a trash bag ringing high up in the trees with bells so fine and small and torn that all we can do, finally, is love them.

Seeing a Lake from Far Away

When I was a boy my family used to drive from Omaha, Nebraska, to northern Michigan every other summer to the glistening blue jewel of Glen Lake up near the village of Empire, where we spent a week or so at our grandparents' cabin. It was a long sixteen-hour journey fraught with its own special kind of dusty and drawn-out longing between rest areas and fanning cornfields, the kind of protracted agony and expectation I've come to associate with the peculiar but lifelong thirst of childhood shot through with bolts of forever, the twinned yearning of some priceless hereafter that can somehow still be had here, albeit in glimpses, shards, and flashes that still occur with sly and surprising frequency at the rise and fall of any lake-bound hill. My parents had no way of knowing what these drives would come to mean to me or how I've been supping on them secretly ever since, as I have never quite gotten over the appalling and heartbreaking sense of anticipation that seeing a lake, our own special, preordained lake, could inspire, especially after not seeing it for a year or more, which could feel like a whole lifetime back then and probably was.

My dad was a cheerful sadist and actor, setting us up repeatedly by asking us if we could see the lake yet as we drove up still another hill knowing full well we had an hour or more to go, the anticipation and following disappointment amounting almost to a low-grade hysteria or religiosity that sometimes

shows up even today almost forty years later whenever I'm
driving to a lake, though in a much more muted and ruminative
form. Of course he knew exactly where we were and how far
away the lake was, and yet he couldn't help himself from fingering the loving wound that he and my mother had bequeathed
to us without ever once announcing it formally, the lifelong
love of lakes that has been so much a part of them as native
Michiganders. They must have taken it for granted in a way, or
couldn't quite understand what the love of lakes could mean
when that same love went unrequited from the very get-go,
growing up in a part of Nebraska that couldn't compete with
Michigan when it came to the number or proximity of lakes
they had been so close to for so much of their formative years.

Those summer trips to Michigan took on an almost mythi-
cal grandeur and meaning in that they had come to represent
a home or even a paradise that I knew just a couple of weeks
out of the year every other year, the rest of my childhood a
kind of landlocked exile far away from this same pellucid and
magical water you could see through all the way to the sandy
bottom, a gift doled out in small doses whose very dearth
caused it to grow bigger in my imagination and daydreams.
And I've always been moved and a little troubled by this, how
these supposedly carefree vacations became a strange species
of soulful and sorrowful sojourn I've never quite recovered
from, as if I'm still grieving for something that was never mine
to begin with whose meaning still eludes my grasp, running
parallel to the collapsing days and even leading me somehow on my own strange journey through life. I had no way
of knowing what was waiting at the end of those long and
delirious drives, that every time I saw the lake for the first time
after a long hiatus I burst into blossom and died a little, that
anything I know of yearning or heartbreak is somehow related

to the sight of this same water, flowing through me as surely
as a current's ribbon coursing through the sun-dappled, rusting metal of a minnow cage.

Who could know this, and who could tell me what it means?

Who could say that seeing the lake for the very first time
would last forever?

Because we can't properly know or anticipate what the sight
of such water will do to us, or how it can somehow sustain us
for a lifetime even as we draw on it as hungry, impoverished
souls when so much is destined to change, the echoes of laughter like so many small waves slapping up against the side of a
teetering dock at twilight. The lake's still there, of course, but
it's like everyone I loved and cherished has somehow slipped
away even as I've slipped away myself, never to return to that
particular place again. So it seems by way of some unfathomable fiat that I've been fairly forced to view the lake and the very
idea of it at a double, even triple remove, for it's been decades
since I was a boy and so much has happened since those first
headlong drives, so much lost and unrequited, with people
flickering in and out like trembling shadows, the seeping and
inevitable undertow of a lifetime, any lifetime, that always takes
away even as it gives anew, no matter what we do or where we
go, no matter how we try to stem the passage of time.

This must be lake knowledge, clear blue water knowledge,
that tends to mystify and obscure through sheer bright
transparency, and it goes so deeply it seems there's no end to
it even as the one who knows it begins to disappear a follicle
at a time. There's nothing heroic or exceptional in this, though
the mystery still abides and continues to sink into ever deeper
strata of awareness, and it's largely because of this same
realization that I've come to know how strangely tragic seeing
a lake can be, though its tragedy is not the stuff of dramatic

action but something infinitely deeper: the tragedy of being
human at all in the face of such beautiful water, the tragedy
that gives us this beauty and then takes it away when we ourselves go under.

For everything else I've come to know about the lake is
somehow secondary to the first sight of it from a distance,
this searing lash of innocence impervious to time because it's
outside time altogether, as fresh, surprising, and heartbreaking
as it ever was or will be, as if the boy who first saw it was given
instantly and forever to know that all such loveliness must end
in the same uncanny and haunting way that one remembers a
certain shaft of sunlight in a pine-scented room, or hears the
sounds of grownups playing cards long after dark as June bugs
zapped the yellow porch lights outside in the telltale crinkling
of a small disaster, these moments and memories the dear-
est things we carry with us throughout a lifetime, though the
moments themselves seem to fade so quickly. Because I can
still see my grandfather's dark tan arm swatting at flies on
the deck even though he has long since passed away, can hear
the boards creaking and sagging as people walked across it
in the signature groan of their own precious weight, can see
the white, lovely sails out on the lake rippling in the wind like
fluted bones, and it's seeing the lake that gives these all to me
even as it takes them away before I ever had a chance to figure
out what they could mean.

So seeing a lake for me is always a slight exercise in the
delicate training of sorrow, even if it is no more felt than the
falling of an eyelash whose impact is nonetheless real, abiding
and essential, bringing us back to the first time we ever saw it
with such eager and innocent eyes. Now in early middle age I
suddenly find myself driving around such lakes alone and looking out over them from the vantage point of one who doesn't

quite know what to do with all of the memories attached to
them, only to report that they are there. And the irony goes
deeper still, because I now live much of my days between two
lakes in a small house out in the woods in northern Michigan
with my wife who knits and sews, and I drive around these
lakes day after day and year after year though I rarely deign
to bathe in them, letting them seep into my waking dreams
and memories to shape me once again into another person
whose first glimpse of heaven came when he and the rest of his
family pulled over that last hill all the way from Nebraska and
could finally see Glen Lake in the distance. It was that precise
moment of seeing the lake for the first time that shot me out
of myself into some other bluer and finer ether dazzling as
free fall, the one I know I am meant to breathe when I can no
longer breathe at all. So I claim this one single instant as the
bridge that spans and connects all others, even the erstwhile
anguish that comes and goes along with all the rest of it. I'm
pointing with my brothers and sisters in the back seat, I'm
open-mouthed and struck dumb with wonder, and I know even
now that no matter what else happens the rest of the way, the
lake will always be there waiting for me to see it for the first
time, the only time, until every part of me is swept up into this
one sustaining gaze.

Why I Go North

I feel it pulling at me at me most days with a strange, tugging insistence as if I'm connected to it by a thin wire made of threadbare light, this sudden desire to drop whatever I'm doing wherever I am and head north alone up Highway 127 until I pass the town of Clare to Roscommon County, where my wife and I have a tiny house out in the woods, a sanctuary I account as the truest, most steadfast haven of my spendthrift life.

But why should this be, exactly?

Why do I continue to feel this almost daily draw and drag as if my soul were so many iron filings magnetized around this one northerly direction that apparently goes on forever? I'm a tabula rasa on the move when I head north, or a child again — I'm one who doesn't know much except that the arc of this same longing trajectory is closer to my one true essence and perhaps everyone's essence after it's all said and done and everything else falls away. I don't understand the fine particulars surrounding the desire to go north and probably never will, not even when I wake from my own death. But who needs particulars when the absolute itself is opening its windows to look out of? Some days I just want to keep going, to cross over Mackinac Bridge into the Upper Peninsula and on up into Ontario until the highways and dirt roads trickle out in the vast tundra of remotest Canada, not even deigning to stop at the North Pole, but venturing farther and farther northward until I'm belly up to the stars.

This is not a responsible compulsion, nor is it anything else that reeks of duty or decorum: it's much deeper and lighter than that, this flight of the alone to the alone, filling the buds of flowers and trees along the way in the ongoing miracle of photosynthesis, the nearly constant temptation not even to flee so much as to truly and finally be, which I'm coming to suspect is a scandal and downright danger to so many in this bustling world. Otherwise, why would this hushed summons feel so sacred and so threatened — why would its solemn giddiness run quietly unchecked throughout me to accompany such headlong movement? All I really know for sure is that a mysterious jettisoning takes place each time I drive north, that ten miles past Mt. Pleasant things begin to fall away of their own mysterious accord without any of my own doing, certain roles and personae and concerns like so many leaves spiraling down from a tree, that in fact I die a little death whose ritual is more than passing strange but which I nonetheless heartily recommend for the staunchest defendants of gregariousness and social obligations, those games we've all learned how to play until they start playing us.

It would seem on the face of it that going north is almost a betrayal or abdication of the most basic calls for community, and yet I cannot but feel that this is nowhere near the whole story, that even these hallowed assumptions have their distortions and shadows that just as often parade under the auspices of a towering and monolithic lie, that any one of us is really who we purport to be when we don our titles or roles no matter how noble or selfless they may appear to be, that we are good citizens or church members or anything else zoot-suited for righteousness.

But when I go north, these somehow have precious little purchase and drop away one by one, not even because I want

them to but because there's just not much to sustain them in
that quiet little house in the woods: they simply can't live in
such relative peace and quiet, not to mention the state roads
and bear-haunted trees, the places I return to again and again
like some wandering tatterdemalion who keeps coming back
to the ground zero of his essential poverty and brokenness,
the anti-qualities that stamp him for the wondering beggar he
truly is. I don't mean to suggest that going north is always even
something I want to do, for in its own way it's a kind of stern
and austere ritual, a gradual unfolding of some interior landscape to match the changing landscape I'm driving through as
northern Michigan comes into its own slow-rising topography
of forests, lakes, and rivers with every kind of growing loveliness in between. It's not always easy to drive to such aloneness,
though in a real way each one of us already is, no matter where
we are or who we're with: we just don't have the requisite space
and silence to know it for ourselves in the marrow of our bones.

So I go north once or twice a week to rediscover this timeless fact and to experience it again anew, I go north in order
to listen and to see and to allow myself to be — I go north less
to live deliberately in the woods than to settle my racing heart
among them so that it may assume once more its proper beat
and rhythm that, who knows, may very well be just another
miniscule echo chamber of the cosmos after all. Besides, each
one of us inherits a universal ache to a greater or lesser degree,
a low-grade and strobing sore that can only be appeased when
we turn to our one true direction and leave everything behind.
I've learned this much in going north, if nothing else.

Now I realize I've been going north all my life, as a twelve-
year-old boy in an Omaha library reading about Peter Freuchen
living among the Eskimos, or listening to the music of Glenn
Gould and learning about his own fascination with the north,

walking into the cold winter winds that swept down from the
Dakotas bringing blizzards in their wake, or even writing at
my desk up north that looks out and faces, you guessed it, a
plumb and drop-dead north. It's not that I harbor any prejudice toward other directions (how preposterous would that
be?), only that at the end of the day and the end of my life the
direction must always point northward, which for all of my
avowals here still carries its fair share of forebodings and even
misgivings, the north's unnerving ability to unsettle. It's like
hearing the music of Arvo Pärt for the first time in its unmis-
takable ringing of eternity, or entering into a vast territory of
silence that keeps opening out onto ever vaster vistas that likewise have their counterparts in me — and so I tend to go north
with a sense of reverence and even awe that's almost laughable
for how much humble ground I cover (it's only seventy miles
away).

I've often wondered in a dim-witted and doubtful way if I'd
ever be able to share this ongoing, seismic attraction and bring
it to the level of utterance, if I'd be able to take the experience of
driving north and offer it to others as a small, chipped talis-
man of the absolute, however meager, however tiny, if this same
palsied tug on the hem of the cosmos could somehow be added
to the long record of other seekers, those who keep going to
ever more remote places because it's somehow inside them to
seek them out. In the end it isn't really a matter of choice and
must be pressed out from within like a fine glacial paste, having
so little to do with will or volition that cannot touch this simple
and profound truth. I don't want to be a hermit or recluse,
though it's true I can't get enough of being near the woods,
of sitting out on the deck and looking at the sky and the trees
and birds that swim inside all of that astonishing ether, for I
truly do feel, like Meister Eckhart, that they are my brothers

and sisters and I'm somehow in paradise with them for hours
at a time, which is all I ever really need to know about living
in this world. It's not the kind of thing one cries out from the
rooftops, this hushed and intimate knowing so sacred that
sometimes even a stone by the side of a dirt road where I walk
or run becomes a friend to me, an ally or lover in being.

But then, almost invariably, the roof of this metaphysical
proclivity caves in, and I become almost afraid: I don't want to
get burned or crucified for going north or feeling the summons
to do so, for admitting to the attraction for such zerohood
where no choir sings or color blings, the continuous subtraction that attends the spanning flight that never ends yet still
contains within it everything that ever was or will be because
it's the void I'm finally talking about here, the drop-away abyss
that makes everything possible and insignificant at the same
time, potential itself falling into fathomless abodes.

Better to be polite and sociable and send Christmas cards,
to pay and mail bills promptly, to keep up on current affairs
and weigh in with one's disapproval and dismay. Leave the
void alone, don't poke it with the needle of the odometer, let it
incubate out beyond the province of zip codes, phone numbers,
platters of salt on the chests of the dead but don't drag even
the mere mention of it into one's living room and office, the
meetings one is already late for. You're an American after all, I
remind myself, an almost dutiful son and husband with trash
to take out — this preoccupation with going north and the
emptiness beyond has no place here, nowhere to set up shop,
and so must cease in service of sociability.

So yes, I can speak in this voice also and feign my belief in
it, I'm a long-accomplished imposter who has mastered the
ability to disguise and ride along the surface with everyone else,
pretending to believe what I do not believe and invest this same

nonbelief with something like Cheerios, knowing all the while that these small traces of north won't leave me alone, that they are in fact constantly tugging at me in subtle ways, pulling on that infinitesimal thread that's connected to the fabric of this life and every life, without exception. It's only when I stop or pause however briefly that I'm able to clear my mind of cant and become aware again that for all of my playacting, the grains of north are gathering all around me, collecting themselves into those same finely shaved filings that will one day sooner or later make the ultimate journey en masse and alone. I see or sense these harbingers of north in the oddest and most unlikely places, an empty shaker on a dining room table turned on its side, the vacant stubble and stare of an old man gazing out a window with his mouth open, rife litter at the back of supermarket near a dented dumpster, a chain-link fence run into by a car.

They point the way but are also somehow the way itself, the greased skids of the infinite that rightly scares the living daylights out of anyone who is rightly lightning struck by them. An icicle hanging from the eaves is north, but so is a drooping shoelace on a Nike dangling from a telephone wire, its woebegone tongue be praised. There's a northern glory in the glowing skeleton of a deer every bit as radiant as any stained-glass cathedral, but you need the eyes of north to see it: I drive through this bone-light church every week and have felt it hum in my innards like a distantly struck chime. Besides, maybe we all have a monk hiding somewhere inside us, kneeling in the dark before a cratered candle and ready to drop everything at a moment's notice. That's what going north does to me, how it goes about its business of steady subtraction.

I used to think this was a character defect I dare not mention, that these solo drives north proved that I'm unsocial, unable or unwilling to abide the presence of others. But then this judgment broke in me as the bad faith and feckless chatter of a desperate bargainer, and I don't even know when or how it happened, only that it did. What I've slowly come to realize is that going north is a kind of preparation, a ritual that is preparing me for what lies beyond even in the midst of such natural splendor, a splendor that cannot be fully understood by anyone, let alone possessed. I'm learning how to die in going north, and at the same time learning how to live. It's teaching me that I don't need very much, that in fact I need nothing very badly — and the more nothingness, the better. So I taste and nibble away at absence, I drink the slow-moving waters of emptiness, and I feel space opening up inside me, space that needs the company of other space, other emptiness. I never considered myself an upright chasm in training, and yet that is exactly what I am — what I think we all are. Who knew such northern exposures weren't anything to be afraid of, that they didn't need to be filled, because it allows everything to pass through it?

This is why I go north so faithfully, and why north has become my stern and loving teacher, though it instructs without saying a single word, without asking anything of me except to go back to it again and again, however feebly, however imperfectly, because in doing so I am somehow released from all the things I'm not, back to that heartbreaking openness that makes everything possible, especially the ability and eagerness to keep on saying yes.

How Gunshots Became a Comfort to Me

My wife and I live much of the year out in the country in a part
of northern Michigan where you can hear gunshots going off
almost every day a couple of miles away out on some lonely,
windswept dunes surrounded by acres of rolling woods. I
know and cherish these dunes because I jog through them off
the gravel state roads that make a righteous, crunching sound
beneath my sneakered feet with every footfall, one of my favorite
sounds in the world and one of the holiest for how it delivers
me back to the earth in a primitive and panting rhythm trickling
out some of the most meaningful steps of my life. The dunes
are moonswept and lovely, as beautiful as a woman's naked hip
as she lay on her side in bed with a curtain waving in the breeze
from a nearby window. But here and there the dunes are littered
with spent casings and shotgun shells along with their riddled
and battered counterparts, woebegone refrigerator doors and
rusting stove tops propped upright, execution style, against one
of the dunes to serve as hapless and makeshift targets.

Where these erstwhile appliances come from I don't know,
and most days when I run by I catch just a fleeting glimpse
of them, wondering less how they came to be there than why
these particular items became the grist for target practice and
not something else, like an old-fashioned archer's bull's-eye,
which I can only infer is due to their squatty and staunch
stature, the regular hollow points and slugs they have to take,

maybe even the particular metallic sound they make when the bullets start ripping into them again. Usually I don't have to contend with gunfire itself so close by, though once in a while I'll run by a lone gunman out on the dunes holding his semi-automatic or sidearm with his trunk lid or tailgate flung wide open as I wave at his startled countenance and realize in some strange, macabre way that he could easily shoot me and dispose of my body quite readily in that relatively remote area, though thankfully no one's tried. I'm sure he must find it equally strange to see someone jogging by out on those bullet-raked dunes, though we're both amiable and cheerful enough, letting the other go back to his particular form of recreation after a brief wave. And it's even stranger to run away at a leisurely pace from a man holding a loaded weapon at my back, to feel him staring after me knowing he could gun me down with a pull of the trigger, though there's also a precious abeyance to it before I reach the top the dunes and disappear from view.

But these brief run-bys aren't the primary way I've come to know these gunshots and their tattooed reports; their staccato refrains find my ears again and again through acres of woods to punctuate my waking dreams and musings to such a degree that they have somehow marked this particular part of the world as much as any birdcall or cresting wave, or the familiar sounds of city traffic to the inveterate urban dweller. No, I've come to slowly know these gunshots in a far subtler and more reluctant way, just as I have the sounds of snowmobiles in winter or the roaring of ATVs in late July or motocross bikes blazing up and down the roads, trailing their own smoking clouds of glory. I think distance and detachment are parts of it, like they are in so many other areas of a more or less quiet and contemplative life.

Now I think there must be some critical distance or thresh-old with gunshots that must be achieved by random or lucky

fiat, say, by a good few miles or so or even farther in order for
these same disturbing sounds to take on a different quality
and timbre, however slightly removed from their bone-jarring
recoils, a claim I make with some misgiving and even disquiet
for what it suggests or indicates, for as we all know in most
other parts of the world gunshots signify only a few possible
brutal outcomes, the death or injury of someone or something
or the peppered destruction of a building's torn-open façade.
But because we live up here in the woods for blessed stretches
of time, I really have no choice but to listen to distant gunshots
and consider what they may mean beyond their obvious and
destructive aim and have even come to accept and embrace them
though I have no interest in joining their rifle- toting numbers.

And this leads necessarily to another consideration I've
had to reckon with almost daily, that I've become a keen and
hypersensitive listener after living so long in loud apartment
buildings working the predawn shift for years loading trucks
at UPS, off the charts for dread when it comes to noise, and
counting off every footstep or muffled voice as if it carried a
funeral march in its wake playing just for me. This is shameful and ludicrous to admit and downright solipsistic, yet it's
one of the deepest personal truths I know, an ongoing and
continuous spell I have yet to break. I don't rightly know where
this hair-trigger predilection for sound comes from or what it
might mean, but it's hunkered down inside me nonetheless and
not going anywhere as far as I can tell. Indeed, it's one of the
most constant and entrenched factors of my life as I largely and
surreptitiously shuffle and arrange my days around different
sounds or lack thereof, pining for the sound of the wind sighing in the trees around our little house up north or that most
beloved and cherished sound of all, the familiar and down-
home cricket chirping unseen from its universal hiding place

under the porch, which has to be one of the wisest and most peaceful sounds ever uttered by any living creature.

But the sound of gunfire a few miles away is something different altogether, though even it has slowly started to change like a movement of the soul that must have its counterpart somewhere in the biosphere. Because so many of the best and clearest hours of my life are spent in a chair leaning over a keyboard and looking out into trees, waiting for the right phrase or word to quietly announce itself, these same telltale gunshots have managed to seep into my entire sensoria, and there's nothing I can do about it but wonder at their deeper significance, if indeed they even have any. Now they no longer conjure just death and destruction but the rat-a-tat percussion sound of the seasons and my own interior life, becoming more pronounced during deer season only to level off almost completely during the coldest winter months. It's strange and moving and a little spooky when the guns fall silent, when for weeks and even months at a time I can't hear anything at all but the ticking of the heat register as I tilt in another direction for the percussive patterns behind my listening. Then it's almost a scandal of silence and has the embarrassing ability to sometimes even bring me to my knees as I fairly slobber in gratitude, listening to the nothing all around fill me up to chin level and rising ever higher.

For in a very profound but absurd way I live my truest life between and among bouts of gunfire going off in the distance, recognizing in them certain signal markers of eternity stretched out between rounds from a magazine clip. This is doubly, even triply strange, because where we live it's possible to go to a gun show three times a month and sometimes even more, and because my dad's own father left all his sons and grandsons more than thirty rifles and revolvers as befitted his Upper Peninsula upbringing, a hardcore country boy if there ever was one, the .30-30 Winchester I chose as a boy after he died having never once been fired and waiting for me even now in the closet like a piece of dark, foreboding patrimony. Once every couple of years I'll take the rifle out and check the action, even hold it up to my chin and aim, admiring the fine craftsmanship and scroll-work that went into the stock, carefully placing it back into its felt-lined case after I have done so with something like nostalgia, though for what time or place I cannot say. I think of the story my dad used to tell of being up in a remote cabin in the UP when they heard a large animal prowling around the door, my grand-father sitting behind it with a locked and loaded shotgun a few feet away, casually smoking one of his beloved Camels, waiting for whatever it was to try to get in so he could open fire.

How could I not but admire his steady poise and find it vaguely troubling at the same time? A fervent and lifelong gun owner, he believed passionately in the right to bear arms, even saw it as essential to being American, and he was never very far from a firearm, a staunch, unwavering belief I wholeheart-edly understand and sympathize with, though I can't endorse it. And yet I sense with every passing year that one of his many gifts to me was an abiding love of nature and reverent observa-tion of the seasons and every kind of wildlife, my grandfather more comfortable fly-fishing or hunting than in any social setting except maybe sitting in a roadside bar. To my everlast-ing surprise I've discovered I'm as much a country boy as he was, though it's taken a quieter and different form. I prefer the garden to the deer blind and walking the trails instead of riding over them, though once in a while it's good to take the Ranger out and drive around four-wheeling, seeing what can be seen from the vantage point of the rocking cab.

There's no special pride or claim to any of this, no peck-ing order of any kind, just one of those honest realizations a person comes to at a certain time in life, at least this one anyway. But I look up sometimes when I hear gunshots in the distance, listening for something both inside and beyond them, listening for something I cannot name. Is peace and well being always a function of remove? Is distance really the soul of beauty, like Simone Weil wrote? What are these shooters practicing to hit anyway, deer or intruders or something that eludes my powers of imagination? I think of children living in war- torn countries or even impoverished parts of major cities across the country and wonder how they must hear gunfire and with what conditioned ears, ashamed almost at what I'm here considering and nearly suffocated by the full implications of it, brought to the brink of an ineffable rage.

Why should any child anywhere have to grow up to the sounds of gunfire for any reason whatsoever? Can anyone really explain it and not resort to rationalization, to the spin of history or socioeconomic theory? And yet even in the asking of these questions I know there are no simple answers, that I myself am implicated in such a world order and so must share my fair part of blame whether I choose to fire a gun or not. People feel the need to own and carry guns and people prac- tice shooting them, people take them out to dunes and fire at scraps of tin and stainless steel that were once used to cook or keep food from going bad: that's all I really know for sure. The rest is speculation, some closer to the truth, some further away. I have to hear the gunshots anyway no matter what personal conclusions I come to, and now I think that how I hear them is important and perhaps even paramount, though why I have such a tilt and hankering I'm not entirely sure.

Some sounds are given us to wrestle with and to ponder in our own way and time, to take back from our waking dreams and nightmares and offer some partial, imperfect report: the rest is not up to us to know or decide. They grow into us like spectral, aural flowers of a troubling beauty and grandeur before they steal away again, tugging at our deepest selves and leaving the lingering imprint of an echo that never truly goes away — or so it is with the gunshots I hear, the hunters and marksmen who continue to provide this haunting and troubling soundtrack behind the sweetest place I have ever known. I'm inside each and every burst of gunfire or the single pistol shot, the rapid series of automatic fire and the high, whistling caliber of a sniper's rifle bullet shot at a playing card taped to a refrigerator door, the ace of spades that will never be dealt again. I listen to these gunshots and I pay attention to them, knowing with a blessed and even towering assurance that one day every gun in the world will fall silent once and for all, never to be fired again, leaving only the sound of the wind in the trees and the least cricket of evening under the porch of a clapboard house, chirping out its one note of everlasting wisdom.

814 V858   **INFCW**

Vivian, Robert,

The least cricket of evening /

CENTRAL LIBRARY

03/12

CPSIA information can be obtained at www.ICGtesting.com
Printed in the USA
BVOW041611080911

270691BV00002B/4/P